Church Wellness

Church Wellness

A Best Practices Guide to Nurturing Healthy Congregations

TOM EHRICH

CHURCH PUBLISHING
an imprint of
Church Publishing Incorporated, New York

Library of Congress Cataloging-in-Publication Data

Ehrich, Thomas L.
   Church wellness : a best practices guide to nurturing healthy congregations
/ Tom Ehrich.
      p. cm.
   ISBN 978-0-89869-597-7 (pbk.)
   1. Church—Marks. I. Title.

   BV601.E37 2008
   253—dc22

                                                                          2008020086

Church Publishing, Incorporated.
445 Fifth Avenue
New York, New York 10016

www.churchpublishing.com

5 4 3 2 1

Contents

Introduction

I DIDN'T KNOW IT AT THE TIME, but this book began in a hotel room in Dallas on an October day in 2003.

In my daily e-mailed "On a Journey" meditation, I asked my 5,000 readers what question they would ask of God. I assumed two things: first, that I would receive only a handful of responses; and second, that they would focus on church-political issues like the upcoming consecration of a gay bishop, ongoing disputes over sexuality and gender, as well as the growing tension between fundamentalist and progressive understandings of Scripture and tradition. I expected anger and frustration.

I was wrong on both counts. Questions flooded into my Outlook inbox. Twenty in the first hour, several hundred in the first few weeks, and, by the time I ended the exercise, some 1,600. I was stunned by the flood of e-mail questions from around the United States and beyond.

Even more, I was disoriented and humbled by their content. Hardly any of the questions concerned church politics. It was the 682nd question that finally mentioned the gay Bishop of New Hampshire. Fewer than 1 percent showed any interest in doctrinal or biblical arguments. In all, the controversies that have been tearing apart mainline denominations accounted for barely 2 percent of questions.

Instead, people wanted to know about God, about the purpose of their lives, about relationships, about suffering, about evil. Their tones were yearning and curiosity, not anger.

As I watched the questions cascade into my inbox, I asked myself: "In eighteen years of preaching every Sunday, how many times did I answer questions that no one was asking?"

I replicated this exercise later that year at several church retreats, just to see if my readership sample had produced a skewed result. Not at all. I asked the same question of Presbyterian clergy in Missouri, Roman Catholic laity in Minnesota, Episcopal parish leaders in Kentucky, and Methodists in Texas. And I got the same results, almost to the exact percentage point.

Next step was to develop a "Listening Church" workshop, in which church leaders focused on listening to the questions that people were asking, rather than assuming they knew or just saying whatever they felt like saying. At one retreat, a top lay official read aloud the questions that his fellow leaders were asking, and by time he finished, he was weeping. It was all so different from what anyone expected.

That work, in turn, led me to do extensive research and writing on what actually contributes to the health of congregations. Maybe we needed to step back from the usual approaches, the standard categories and ideas, and to think with a radical freshness.

This book represents what I discovered. I have no doctrinal axes to grind, no denominational (or anti-denominational) agenda to pursue. I simply yearn for health in congregations. In my opinion, a healthy congregation is a thing of great beauty and grace. It can make a difference in its community and enable its constituents to make a difference with their lives.

Rather than continue stale discussions that haven't yet yielded good fruit, I think we should look at the factors that actually contribute to congregational health. Rather than perpetuate stale methods, we should look at what works. What are the "best practices" that tend to produce good results?

I don't want to be simplistic. I know that all institutions resist change and health. Churches show strong devotion to practices that haven't worked for decades, if indeed they ever worked.

But neither do I want to avoid reality. Ineffective practices are costly, in dollars, in lost opportunity, and in frustration. An unhealthy congregation ends up hurting its members. A less-than-optimal congregation can miss important opportunities to serve and can risk future decline.

The concept of "church wellness" doesn't start with an assumption of sickness. Rather, it starts in a belief that any congregation can become healthier, and that congregations want to be healthy. Other than a few partisans who will sacrifice anything, even their beloved church, to win the victory of right opinion, most church members want to be part of a congregation that is serving effectively, growing, responding to people's questions, and leading people deeper in their faith.

I am grateful to the many church leaders who helped me to think through these best practices. I continue to be amazed by how passionately people care about their congregations and how, in numbers greater than we might think, people are ready to move on, to embrace better ways, and to seek better days.

Overview

THE CHURCH WELLNESS PROJECT is a "best practices" guide to nurturing a healthy faith community. My focus is on the basics. In the Seven Key Factors that determine congregational health, I offer guidance on specific steps to be taken. I have no doctrinal or denominational axes to grind. My only purpose is to help congregations be as healthy as they can be.

The Seven Key Factors that shape congregational health are:

1. Membership Development
2. Leadership Development
3. Communications Strategy
4. Spiritual Development
5. Young Adults Ministries
6. The Listening Church
7. Metrics

WHAT ARE "BEST PRACTICES"?

The Church Wellness Project is built on the concept of "best practices," a widely accepted concept in fields ranging from medicine to auto sales. Briefly, the concept means that some methods and processes are better—more effective, more productive, more likely to achieve desired ends—than others.

In medicine, for example, complicated surgical procedures tend to follow widely accepted best practices. In sales, best practices include prompt response to inquiries, consistent follow-through on commitments, and tracking interactions with prospects and customers. In singing, it is a best practice to do stretching and vocal exercises before rehearsing or performing. When an entrepreneur signs up with a franchise, he or she typically receives a "playbook" containing best practices for running a successful enterprise.

The same is true in congregational life. To attain health, a congregation needs to adopt the best possible practices for doing its basic work. With some allowance for context, it is possible to name best practices for such basic tasks as greeting visitors, handling church communications, training leaders, and serving young adults.

If best practices are consistently employed in the Key Factors affecting congregational health, the congregation will tend to be healthy and to function effectively. Conversely, if best practices are ignored, and suboptimal or even wrongheaded practices are employed, the congregation will have great difficulty attaining health.

Adopting best practices isn't easy or automatic. In any enterprise, even religion, best practices change over time, as contexts change and new methods emerge, and resistance to best practices runs deep. Many people cling to inherited ways even when they demonstrably fail to work, because those ways are familiar, confer certain privileges, and have been deemed ideologically "correct."

In the Church Wellness Project, our premise is that many congregations want health and effectiveness, if only because years of decline have driven them to the edge of survival, and are willing to let go of practices that aren't optimal. Further, we think more congregations are ready to measure their efforts and to be guided by outcomes.

WHAT DO WE MEAN BY "WELLNESS"?

"Wellness" in a church doesn't mean anything as simple as 98.6 degrees on a thermometer. But we can discern some signs of "wellness" in a faith community. They include:

- growth in membership
- vibrant mission work that makes a discernible difference in the larger community
- members' lives being transformed
- congregation able to take risks, fail without recrimination, and learn from failure
- transparency and confidence in dealing with conflict
- ablility to deal creatively with change
- open communications
- members bringing their yearnings and questions to church
- leaders willing to be guided by outcomes.

Wellness is dynamic, not a steady state that a congregation reaches and then maintains. Wellness lies in how a faith community responds to change, stress, opportunity, failure, and people's needs and personalities.

HOW DO WE CHOOSE WHERE TO START?

Energy will follow need and interest. Even though, from a practical standpoint, you could start anywhere and build toward a balanced program, your most pressing needs will be a reasonable starting point.

Many congregations, for example, are concerned about declining membership. Membership Development, therefore, will respond to felt needs. At other congregations, where membership seems too "gray" for long-term vitality, a focus on Young Adults Ministry might make more sense.

Two points to consider:

First, in order to assess your efforts, you will need measures of what is working or not working. Therefore, some attention to Metrics will be necessary wherever you start.

Second, virtually any best practices that you choose to implement will require a capable web site to be effective. While you work on, say, Membership Development or Leadership Development, it would be good to have a parallel effort to implement a portion of the Communications Strategy section, namely, a web site that uses best practices in design and features and an Internet-based communications system.

Remember, finally, that your starting point is exactly that, a starting point, not a full project.

HOW DO WE MAKE A PLAN?

Any plan involves guesswork and intention, as well as the specific first steps to take.

People like to think they can do more than that, perhaps even plan an entire campaign. Plans, however, have a way of unraveling as intention encounters resistance, and guesswork encounters reality. The best plan, therefore, focuses on:

- next steps to take
- resources needed
- who will be responsible
- measures of success or failure in next steps
- process for planning further steps.

One principle is known as S.A.M. = Specific, Attainable, and Measureable. A good plan commits specific people to take specific actions by specific dates and using specific resources. Each step should be reasonably attainable, although resistance and other factors will come into play. And measurements matter. A vague plan—"Let's grow our church!"—isn't helpful.

Effective planning needs to be open and transparent, so that the wisdom of dissenting voices can be heard, and the people who will be expected to pay for the plan, to staff it, and to endure its dislocations have an opportunity to be part of the planning. Remember the old saw: "People tend to support what they helped to create." At the same time, remember that over-ambitious plans can paralyze a congregation. It is important that a few key leaders have a sense of the over-arching trajectory, but that they remain flexible even as shorter-term and smaller steps are taken.

Remember to learn from failure, not to use failure as an occasion for blame. Churches in particular need to stop pouncing on failure as an excuse to stop change.

HOW DO WE WORK OUR PLAN?

As another old saw puts it, "Sooner or later, every good idea degenerates into work." The working of a plan means effort expended and measurements taken.

Some keys to working a plan:

* Transparency is critical. In order to trust the plan and its impact, people in the congregation need to know what is going on, by whom, to what end, and on what schedule.
* Timetables and deadlines are helpful. Church work competes with other work in people's lives. If reminded of a deadline, church workers are more likely to make time available for church work.
* Sequencing needs to be thought out. Some actions are prerequisites for others. Some actions need to be tested before others can proceed.

- Accountability, not blaming, is necessary. If someone fails to carry out a task and isn't held accountable for it, the word goes out, "This doesn't matter." Accountability also is a kindness to the person who dropped the ball. It frees them to apologize or to explain and to feel acceptable for future work, even if they need to bow out of this specific assignment.

TIPS ON PLANNING

A good Church Wellness plan is like a baseball player running the bases.

- If you don't get to first base, you're out. No lolly-gagging.
- As you near first base, your base coach tells you whether to stop or try for second.
- Proceeding on, conditions are changing rapidly, so listen to the next base coach.
- Be prepared to stop, for another batter is coming up.

When we believe in a venture and are impatient to see it succeed, we are tempted to plan too much. We build too many untested assumptions into later stages, and we fall in love with our plan. The numbers and dates add up, and at the end, we have "scored a run."

In fact, life is too dynamic for that. So are organizations. Any first step we take will provoke multiple responses, some positive, some negative. Outcomes will include successes and disappointments, not to mention surprises. The context for continuing becomes increasingly fluid.

Continued

In effective organizational planning,

- First-stage plans need to be specific, attainable, and measurable.
- Later-stage plans need to be flexible, responding to outcomes and not clinging to expectations and intentions.

Thus, a first-stage will look like this:

- Train lay callers to visit all first-time Sunday visitors on the day of their first visit.
- Equip them with a data-gathering tool for measuring impact and planning follow-up.

A second-stage will look like this:

- If visitors welcome home visits on Sunday, keep doing them. If feedback is a preference for mid-week call at work, or only a phone call, change methods.
- If lay visitors report positive experiences, keep assigning them. If they report negative experiences, learn from their experience and either select new callers or modify the calling plan.

As you can see, the farther out you get, the more you need to be guided by outcomes, not original intentions.

In the Church Wellness Project, we offer a generalized road-map, which is based on three assumptions about church planning:

- Build on small successes, and thereby grow in confidence.

Continued

- Listen to your congregation and to the metrics you established.
- Be prepared to revise at every stage.

WHO SHOULD CARE ABOUT WELLNESS?

One challenge in promoting Church Wellness is recognizing it as work for many hands, and as a project whose success touches the entire body, not just paid staff and key volunteers. If a congregation means anything to its various members, then the congregation's wellness is properly their concern. For, whatever their level of interest, a healthy church will respond to their yearnings and needs, whereas an unhealthy church will frustrate them and often hurt them.

We recognize, of course, that church means different things to people. A few care intensely about its day-to-day workings. A larger group sees the church as a central part of their lives. An even larger group turns to church for occasional worship, life-transition sacraments, and help in time of need. And a final group considers themselves members but asks little of the church. Or, from another perspective, some see church as the locus of their faithful servanthood in the world, whereas others serve separately from church but still see themselves as Christians doing mission. Some have active spiritual lives that only occasionally touch down in Sunday worship or teachings.

None of these participation modes is better than another. But one thing is clear: if the local church is weak, incapable of making wise decisions, inattentive to persons, heavy-handed in imposing obligation but oblivious to listening, over-controlled by a core group, a battleground for doctrine or lifestyle issues, and improvident in managing its common life, then every level of engagement suffers.

How does a self-identified "core group" member dedicate his or her life to an institution that isn't worthy of devotion? How does a twice-monthly worshiper find any sustenance in a lifeless assembly? How does a "Christmas-and-Easter Christian" find those life-changing stories in a prickly, self-serving body more concerned about money and avoiding change than about touching lives for God?

In the Church Wellness Project, we assume that the first expression of interest will come from a pastor who is eager to lead his or her congregation to a better place, or a lay leader who sees possibilities. But it is our hope that many members will access these materials and develop a keen and informed interest in Church Wellness.

In caring about Church Wellness, a few will dig deeply into the nuts-and-bolts of congregational life and work with paid staff to adopt "best practices" in every critical area. A larger group won't attend planning sessions, but they will give permission for best practices to be implemented, even though some things might change. Thus, many in the congregation can play some part in improving the health of the church.

CHAPTER

Membership Development

MANY CONGREGATIONS will start here, because they want to build a vibrant, durable, and growing community of members and they realize that without intentional effort to retain current members and to recruit new members they will stall and eventually die.

Membership Development requires fresh thinking and special attention to best practices. Many congregations have inherited or fallen into membership-related habits that are undermining other efforts. Here are some basic concepts in effective membership development:

1. Balance and Energy

   Effective Membership Development is BALANCED and ENERGETIC. Balanced means focused on retention and recruitment and transformation—not just one, but all three. Energetic means putting forth a sustained and consistent effort, rather than the occasional grand gesture.

2. Retention

   RETENTION of current members is the foundation for ongoing community and activity. Retention efforts aim at keeping members engaged in church life, at a level of involvement that is consistent with their needs and interests. As they say in business, "The easiest sale to make is to the customer you already have." A "repeat customer" is a satisfied customer who perceives involvement as rewarding and worth continuing.

3. Recruitment

   RECRUITMENT of new members compensates for normal loss of members due to transitions such as death and new jobs, provides fresh energy and ideas, keeps the congregation in touch with its larger community, and fulfills the Great Commission given by Jesus to "make disciples."

4. Transformation

   TRANSFORMATION means going deeper in one's faith, making life choices that reflect one's faith, and allowing one's life to change and one's values to become more aligned with God. The aim isn't conformity, but repentance, or change of mind. Just belonging to a congregation isn't enough. Just claiming a Christian label isn't enough. Faith must lead to newness of life. Transformation can proceed by many pathways, but one consistent characteristic will be change.

5. Service

   A healthy congregation is proactive about SERVING its members, not passive in waiting for them to complain. Serving members doesn't necessarily mean pleasing them. Much of the Gospel is challenging, chastening, and confusing. So is life. A healthy congregation will have tears, disagreements, resistance, and "grinding of teeth." But those strains will happen in response to the Gospel, not in response to the institution's weakness or orneriness.

6. Funds

   Although some FUNDS are required for membership development, the heart of it is work done by persons in an organized program the components of which are transparent to all. Best practices aren't usually expensive. Poor practices tend to be quite costly.

7. Resistance

   RESISTANCE to growth must be addressed firmly and openly, not apologetically. Jesus formed open circles, not closed societies. When one person or group imposes its self-interest on the whole as an argument against growth or change, it compromises the church's future and violates God's trust. The pain caused by growth and change must be addressed as a pastoral need, not as a reason to stand still or to erect barriers.

8. Transparency

   TRANSPARENCY is critical. Members need to know what is being done and why, whether efforts are succeeding, and how the body is being affected. New members need to be introduced, for example. Membership statistics must be accurate and available to all.

RECRUITMENT AND RETENTION AND TRANSFORMATION

Church growth worth pursuing requires a balance among recruitment and retention and transformation. It does no good to bring a hundred new members in the front door while you push a hundred longtime members out the back door. Nor does it do any good to be so focused on serving the members you have that you leave no room, heart, or resources for welcoming new members. Nor does growth endure if nothing changes in a member's life. In the end, counting those who belong means less than sending a cadre of committed, restored, forgiven, refreshed, and mercy-giving believers into a challenging world.

Balancing recruitment and retention and transformation isn't easy. One challenge, of course, is the tendency of any group to "pull up the drawbridge" behind it. They have worked their way in, found their niche and friendships, and now they want to prevent any further growth and change that might threaten what they have. All groups do this, from immigrants to suburbanites to office workforces to churches. It's self-defeating, but that doesn't stop groups from doing it.

Another challenge is that recruitment ministries are quite different from retention ministries as stages in an incorporation process, and transformation work is different yet again. To do all three, you need to plan carefully and operate transparently. For example, recruitment entails a warm and public "welcome," whereas retention focuses on small groups and deepening relationships. Transformation, in turn, happens through solid content, life-changing mission, the challenge of self-examination.

Recruitment assumes a need to explain everything, from how worship proceeds to where bathrooms are located. Retention, on the other hand, encourages people to feel a certain on-board comfort—this is my church, and I know my way around it. Transformation, by contrast, entails an awareness that I am changing and therefore not fitting in as easily anywhere, even here in church.

Recruitment occupies a lot of clergy time, whereas retention, if done properly, transfers care-giving and support to small, lay-led groups. Transformation involves the entire community.

Recruitment tends to stay near the surface, because the deeper questions that motivate us aren't in focus or don't yet feel safe. Retention, on the other hand, yearns to go deeper, even to the border of transformation and beyond. The deeper questions and the venues they encourage, such as retreats and healing ministries, might seem frightening to newcomers. The what-am-I-doing-here questions of newcomers might seem shallow to longtime members.

Balancing these ministries is hard on clergy. To be crass about it, existing members are paying the bills and expect to be served, but if the pastor doesn't tend aggressively to recruitment ministries, there will be no future. When people vie for the pastor's time, it is essential that top lay leaders step in and say to the congregation, "Our mission is growth. Without growth we die. Let's work together to let growth happen."

RETAIN CURRENT MEMBERS

Retention of current members is critical to the overall health of the congregation. In an age of high mobility, declining "brand loyalty," and competing interests, the healthy congregation will work hard to retain its members, using these best practices:

Learn Members' Needs

If you know your members' actual needs, you can serve them effectively. If you don't know those needs, your efforts can seem insincere, obtuse, or irrelevant. Members' actual needs are constantly changing, as their lives and circumstances change; ministries that served them well a year ago might not be pertinent today. Members' actual needs tend to be diverse and not easily served by single-shot ministries. Identifying and implementing pertinent ministries require you to overcome certain obstacles.

One obstacle is projection, which occurs when ministry planners project their own interests or needs onto others. Another is assumption, when ministry planners assume they know what others need. Further obstacles include inertia and habit, which lead to continuing to offer yesterday's ministries without verifying that they still are pertinent. Finally, constituencies develop around certain ministries that insist on perpetuating older ministries and blocking new ministries.

Such obstacles are inevitable in any institution. But they must be overcome. Otherwise, the congregation falls farther and farther behind in recognizing, assessing, and responding to actual needs. To overcome such resistance, you need data on what needs exist that aren't being addressed.

Needs identification process

Personally calling on members to inquire about their needs accomplishes two purposes: it identifies their needs and it strengthens their sense of belonging. This needs to be a personal encounter, not a survey form, and it should be made by a trained caller who listens and makes connections. The connections matter as much as the data they yield. The inquiry focuses on the member's life, not on his or her desire to participate in existing programs. This isn't about selling or defending current offerings.

Each caller should receive training in how to ask a leading question and then listen to the answer, and how to avoid problem-solving, therapy, or being invited into a conflict. This is a time to listen, not to fix. Callers will have a few standard starter questions, but should feel free to improvise. The point is to listen, not to fit members' sharing into preconceived patterns. Starter questions can include:

- "Please bring me up to date on life in your family." (Listen especially for changes, difficulties, joys.)
- "How does this coming year look to you?"
- "Do you find yourself (or your partner, children, parents) asking specific questions of God?"

The caller will want to avoid church-directed questions, such as "What can your church do for you?" Or "How do you feel about your church?" There is a place for such questions, but the needs-identification process should focus on the member and be less channeled into church programing.

In preparing for the annual visit, callers need to be equipped with information about likely cultural and community trends. Threatened closure of a local factory, for example, should lead callers to listen for signs of economic distress. Recent newspaper articles about drugs and violence in schools could signal shifts in parents' confidence. Callers should be mindful of larger cultural trends, such as rising medical costs, declining real estate values, growing anonymity, or a spike in crime.

Data-sharing. It is important that pastoral staff (clergy and designated lay ministers) be informed of significant pastoral needs. The larger task for the Needs Identification team is to capture as much information as possible about members, so that the data can be queried to identify emerging needs, unmet needs, and overall demographic trends.

Whether or not a data survey form is used in visiting members—I think forms tend to create barriers—members' responses do need to be turned into data.

Ideally, a database professional will work with your team to design tables for storing data, a series of reports based on known queries, and a process for doing ad hoc queries, including keyword searches.

Anecdotal information—people's stories—has great value in a church setting. These stories reveal additional insights into trends and needs.

Look for Patterns. In general, Needs Identification is concerned with identifying patterns to which the church can respond, not an assessment of past offerings. For example, year-to-year growth in the population of children will tell you about future space requirements, future educational needs, programs for young parents, as well as whom these families are likely to bring to church. Growth in divorced singles tells a different story and suggests need for support groups and social networking. If loneliness is discerned, you will want to understand whether it is related to age, relocation, change in life, or personal trauma such as job loss or death of a partner.

Look especially for emerging needs. They are an indication of where God is leading you.

Because such needs are new, they can be difficult to discern. However, if you wait for an emerging need to have a "critical mass" sufficient to gain traction and to overcome resistance, it might be too late. Understand that members' search usually is for depth and meaning, not just friendships or belonging, and not church activity.

After World War II, newly mobile families sought out churches as a way to get grounded in new communities. That behavior has ended. People tend to have other avenues to socialization, such as workgroups and gyms. They don't look to church for purely social friendships. The exception might be in very large cities, where workgroups are less likely to coalesce into friendships.

Church promises depth, meaning, spiritual friends, belonging in something significant. That means it might not be enough to sponsor, say, a Valentine's Dance, whereas a mission-minded dance to raise funds for a Habitat House would fulfill a need for "fun with a purpose."

Belonging habits have changed, too. At one time, people tended to identify themselves by where they went to church. In most of the U.S., that has ceased to be the case. Church promises belonging in something transformational. That rarely has to do with brand or label, but with a specific community of people who are engaged in faith activities that seem significant.

Respond to actual needs

If you respond to actual needs, you will make a difference in people's lives and win their loyalty. On the other hand, if you ask members to fit their needs into existing offerings, or expect them to stifle their needs as the price of belonging, you will serve them poorly and discourage loyalty.

Personal needs require personal response. Of all institutions, the church has both the opening and the obligation to make a personal response to people's needs. People endure anonymous and mechanical responses from other institutions. They expect more from a faith community.

With some exceptions, most church members will grant their church access to their lives. They will respond to personal visits, telephone calls, e-mails, and letters. In a need situation, they probably won't respond to a broadside invitation, such as, "If anyone needs a personal visit, call the church office."

"Personal" can mean an e-mail or phone call, as well as a face-to-face encounter.

Ministers (lay and clergy) need to tailor their response to the need, not to their own personal preferences and availability. A grief situation, for example, requires a personal visit. A job promotion can be handled with a personal e-mail or letter. A job loss, by contrast, requires a call or visit. Better to err on the side of doing too much than too little.

People need to be "sold." They aren't looking for one more activity to fill their schedules, or one more list to send them canned appeals, not even well-intended appeals like "call us if you have a need" or "come to church for a support group." People need to be approached personally, by name, with a sense that their participation matters and is somehow tied in with a recognition of who they are.

By making a personal contact, you can learn right away whether your assessment of needs is accurate. This is better than investing resources in a "good idea" that has no grounding in actual needs.

Being on a prayer list isn't substitute for a pastoral call. Clergy need to develop the habit of making pastoral calls other than in hospital emergencies. Personal calls build goodwill, establish one's ministry, elicit members' stories, needs, and interests, and strengthen their affiliation with the congregation. Pastoral calls are time-consuming and difficult to schedule, but unless clergy know their people, how can they serve them? When a person has needs, personal attention from a pastor will make far more difference than being mentioned on the prayer list or receiving a pretty card. Clergy need to be the primary caller, but they can ask trained laity to assist.

Informal care-giving networks also exist within a congregation, and they make an enormous difference. Small group ministries are especially important. Also important are teams of intentional care-givers, such as Stephen Ministers.

Clergy should plan on making a personal visit with every parish family once a year. They should respond to emergencies as they arise and plan on visiting hospitalized patients at least once a week. Lay callers should visit the hospitalized more frequently (being guided by medical circumstances) and shut-ins (homebound and retirement centers) at least once a month. This is a lot of calling, but it will make a difference in people's lives and cement their loyalty to the congregation.

Callers need to be flexible about where and when a call is made. Few people below retirement age are at home during the day. Lunch near a member's job can be a good approach, as can breakfast, mid-morning coffee, meeting after work at a watering hole, or Saturday lunch after a kid's soccer game. The point is to show interest in people's lives.

Design programs that fit perceived needs. Programs should show transparency: you spoke, we listened; or, you had a need, we responded. Change offerings regularly, stay fresh, avoid programs that people "stop seeing." Programs should seek to help people, not to promote the church as an institution. Fewer fundraisers, fewer church-planning sessions, and more mission groups, pastoral groups, and study groups. Offer one-time events (such as a seminar on prayer) to gauge interest and to identify follow-up opportunities.

Market effectively

The marketing of any church program must compete with other marketing efforts around us. It doesn't need to be a slick or hard sell, but it does need to show purpose and confidence.

In general, we need to stop relying on verbal announcements on Sunday morning and notices pinned to bulletin boards. Those are low-impact tools. Instead, use targeted e-mails and your e-mail newsletter to market programs. Maintain categorized member data to support targeted marketing. In marketing a program, be sure to include:

- intended audience
- intended benefits from participation
- schedule
- leadership
- cost (if any)
- prerequisites (if any), such as daytime availability, special skill, prior experience
- an easy way to ask questions (such as an e-mail reply link)
- an easy way to register (such as via web site).

Afterward, use e-mail tools to solicit feedback—on the suitability of this offering, on execution, and on needs for further offerings. Engage in dialogue with members rather than trying to guess what they will support.

Provide different commitments and multiple ways in

Ministry planners must allow for different levels of commitment and provide multiple avenues of engagement.

Congregations tend to have at least four levels of commitment:

- core groups (church is center of their lives)
- active members (participate regularly, take leadership roles, don't "live and breathe" church)
- occasional members (worship once a month or less, participate in programs that meet their needs, rarely accept leadership roles)
- infrequent members (worship on high holidays, come to a few events, identify themselves as members of the congregation, but rarely participate).

Each level of commitment is acceptable. Core groups need to stop seeing their high commitment level as normative for all. Active members need to stop trying to "fix" the inactive by luring them toward the center.

Each level of commitment requires unique activities and offerings; one size doesn't fit all.

All need to be seen as rewarding and significant. Avoid suggesting a hierarchy of activities. Ad hoc and annual events matter, too. Avoid setting high participation as a universal standard, rather, let people find their way according to their needs.

Establish a visible gatekeeper, a clearly identified leader and norm-setter, who is accessible. Make that person available via your web site. Route inquiries to the gatekeeper, rather than to staff, thereby avoiding staff bottlenecks.

In general, people need to be invited to join a ministry or event, and not just informed that it is occurring. The common appeal—"If you'd like to come, see . . ."—does little to encourage participation. It comes across as lazy. A personal invitation makes people feel that their participation will be appreciated.

Two rules of thumb: people tend to support what they helped to create, and people tend to value what they paid for. Helping to create can include serving on a planning team, but also responding to a survey, taking a poll in the church newsletter, or serving on a focus group.

Pre-registration is helpful in estimating attendance. It also provides a way to collect a fee—whether a token fee or actual cost of materials and/or food—and thereby to encourage attendance.

Track participation

Systematic efforts to track participation will pay off over time. You will learn which events were marketed effectively, which responded to actual needs, and which members (or groups of members) were served and which were ignored. The best way to track participation is with a database-driven tracking system.

Actual data will be more helpful than vague memories or impressions. As the Metrics section explains, your best guide to program management will be actual data on how many participated and who they were.

Not all activities can be expected to draw a large crowd. But you can state expectations, measure actual vs. expected results, and then compare year to year. You also want to look for diversity of participation. If the same handful of people attend every event, your offerings need to be more diverse and need to be marketed more effectively.

A useful database need not require advanced technical skills. An Excel spreadsheet can work, so can a simple database using

Microsoft Access. The point is to capture the data and not leave it to memory.

You want to track both numbers (expected vs. actual) and names of persons. In a relational database, you can draw correlations such as which age ranges attended a certain event, gender breakdown, or length of tenure as a factor. You can discern trends, such as consistently low attendance at new member events despite a large number of new members. Once you know to whom you need to reach out, it will be time to look at marketing.

Anticipate end-points for specific activities

Most groups, events, or programs benefit from having a stated end-point. Churchgoers tend to resist open-ended commitments, both as leaders and as participants. An end-point helps to shape the activity's trajectory. It provides a recognized time for expressing gratitude. If a program has been poorly led or attended, an end-point provides a graceful exit. Even poor ideas have constituencies. Some people will want a failed program to continue because it meets their needs, even though it drains resources that could be channeled to other ideas. Leaders who are responsible for allocating limited resources need a way to terminate a program without offending its constituents.

Initiate recruitment for ministry

With few exceptions, people need to be recruited personally for ministry in the congregation, not pointed to a "signup sheet" or invited vaguely to "see Bob after worship." This is especially true if your goal is to broaden participation beyond a small group of regulars.

Personal means personal. The best recruitment is done by personal telephone call, a face-to-face meeting, a personal letter, or a personal e-mail (not a broadcast e-mail).

Such methods require more work, and they require exposure to the risks associated with personal interaction, including the risk of rejection. Moreover, asking someone to serve requires the asker to understand why the invitation is being made to this person. It is easier and safer not to take those risks. It is time to move beyond the "warm body" approach—"Anyone who wants . . ."—because it dishonors both the ministry and the audience. Instead, best practice is to think through the work to be done, to consider who in the congregation is well suited to do it, to make sure the same few capable people aren't being overloaded, and to approach targeted individuals.

Most ministries require at least some training. Some require substantial training. Best practice is to anticipate the need for training and not assume that informally transmitted lore will be sufficient. Recruitment for ministry is an important opportunity to strengthen performance by signaling value and by equipping the minister.

Ask regularly, as needs and situations change. This is where a database can be useful. People often need to decline an opportunity to serve, but the nuance of their declining needs to be noted. It could be, "not this time, but please ask me again," or it could be, "I'm not the least interested in taking on any ministry."

If one ministry wasn't suitable—too time-consuming, too complex, presents a schedule conflict—another ministry might be welcome. Also, situations change, and a time-stressed member might have more time after job loss or retirement, or as young children become more self-sufficient.

Provide customer service

As businesses discover, "customer service" cannot be left to chance or to antiquated tools. Clearly marked pathways for stating needs and securing information are critical for retaining current members.

People need help and information. In any organization, especially in busy times when people participate in multiple organizations, people need help in navigating institutional life, obtaining information, making specific requests, voicing complaints and concerns, and accessing services.

What seems simple to some can feel awkward and foreign to others. What "everyone knows" usually proves to be known by only a few (such as how to donate flowers at Easter). This is especially true for unusual needs (such as relocating an aging parent), for needs that arise in traumatic periods (such as after death), and for needs that tend to be invisible to the congregation's mainstream (such as dealing with sexual abuse).

Complaints matter. They matter to the members, for a negative experience that isn't voiced or heard can fester and come out later as passive-aggressive undermining. Better to provide avenues for transparent and direct voicing of issues. Complaints matter to the congregation, too. They signal unmet needs, inadequate performance, or hurtful situations. Those negatives need to be addressed. The congregation needs to be known as responsive, not defensive or resistant.

"Customer service" requires size-sensitive planning. All congregations need multiple avenues for seeking help and information. Informal conversations on Sunday aren't sufficient for even the smallest congregation. Nor is it sufficient to depend on a brief comment to the pastor or a lay leader. The larger the church, the more comprehensive its customer service system needs to be. The available tools need to be clearly identified and easy to use.

That means, first, web-based tools: links on the congregation's web site that open an e-mail form, a "frequently asked questions" section, a listing of contact persons for various situations, and an invitation to telephone or make an appointment. The e-mail form should identify a trusted person (pastor, church secretary, senior lay leader) as recipient for sensitive inquiries, or a relevant person for informational inquiries.

- E-mail should be acknowledged immediately and answered the same day.

- Telephone calls during normal business hours should be answered by a person, not a machine. Businesses with a strong commitment to customer service are abandoning automated systems. The church should do no less. People don't call the church to deal with menus, to punch telephone buttons, or to leave messages on voice-mail. They call to talk to someone.

- Personal contacts should be encouraged but managed. If the clergy are going to have time available for pastoral calls, for study and preparation, and for their families, they need to manage on-site time effectively. Certainly, in an emergency, a drop-in visit is appropriate. Otherwise, members should be trained to make appointments and be told why. Best practice is to design a transparent system that is fair to all and doesn't expose the clergy to charges of being aloof or unavailable.

- Prompt response is essential. Whatever tool is used, best practice is to acknowledge immediately and to respond within the same day. The response might be a promise to reply later, but some response must be made.

- A tracking system can be helpful, especially in larger congregations. Keeping track of requests and responses made and promised can exhaust the memory of even the most devoted staff members. Tracking also signals patterns, suggests a need for more available information, and indicates adequacy of staffing. Any decision to add or to eliminate staff positions needs to have data behind it, not just vague impressions.

- Clear accountability is critical for nurturing trust. Every organization makes mistakes. So does every person. People are highly tolerant of faulty systems or fallible persons, as long as the "customer" doesn't encounter denial, defensiveness, or hostility.

RECRUIT NEW MEMBERS

Recruitment of new members is critical not only to a congregation's survival, but to a lively sense of purpose and an energetic engagement with the world as well.

In this section we deal with best practices for responding to a potential member and incorporating them into the congregation.

Recruitment includes:

- evangelizing (helping converts to make a commitment to Jesus Christ)
- re-engaging (helping lapsed members to gain fresh interest in Christian community)
- welcoming (embracing persons who are new to town or seeking a new church home).

Customer Evangelism

The most effective evangelism occurs when one person tells another about God or about a church where God is alive.

Word of mouth has an authenticity that advertising campaigns cannot equal. There is no better "sales person" than a satisfied "customer." Your first and best step in encouraging positive word of mouth is giving members something positive to talk about with their friends.

Be proactive about encouraging authentic positive word of mouth. For example, schedule events to which satisfied customers can invite friends. Form open-door groups, classes, and community-service activities that will welcome a member's friend.

Conversely, negative word of mouth from a dissatisfied "customer" can undermine your best efforts. Don't let negative word of mouth go unnoticed. Hold open forums for addressing issues. Make a public commitment to address problems, then provide a tangible way to express a problem, such as an "Ask the pastor" link on an e-mail newsletter. Some negative word of mouth is intended to be destructive and must therefore be challenged. Some contains important clues about unmet needs, inadequate systems, or underperforming staff, and must therefore be heard.

Web Tools

Make high-quality invitational materials available via the web for members to forward to friends. Provide web site tools that enable members to add friends to your church's e-mail list for newsletter and targeted messages. (For example, a Young Adults list for invitations and news especially suitable for Young Adults.) On your e-mail newsletter, include a "Forward to a Friend" button. In the Internet age, so-called "viral marketing" happens when people pass around ideas and information. One key method is forwarding an e-mail or document to one or many friends. A convenient forwarding link enables a brief moment of enthusiasm to initiate action.

Street-visibility is Overrated

One of my favorite churches is erecting a new sign along a busy city street. It will be large, expensive and, they hope, readable at 45 MPH. They expect the sign to draw people into the church and thereby help them to reverse a long slide in membership. If they had asked me, I would have said skip the sign and put your money into improving your e-mail newsletter. That newsletter is your "visibility," not your buildings or signs.

People hear about churches, they don't read property signs. They can find where the church is located—put a map on your web site, that's where they will look—but they must want to know. That wanting won't be impacted by a sign, but by a "customer evangelist" who says powerful things about his church, or by a school that has a good reputation, or by strong newsletters that members forward to friends.

Taking care of property is something a church does for the self-esteem of its members, not to attract new members. Instead of a sign, plant a flower garden, which reminds members to appreciate beauty. Better still, start a Wednesday program—a midweek evening when people gather for table fellowship and group activities such as classes and support groups—with an exciting program and room for strangers. Instead of a wooden or stone sign, start a transformational mission program, and let that be a "sign" of your congregation's values.

Respond to Visitors

Before you strategize about how to increase the flow of visitors, you need to craft a detailed plan for responding effectively and consistently to visitors, especially on the Sunday of their first visit.

Numerous best practices for responding to visitors are well known. What is often missing is a sense of urgency about managing this vital ministry well. A good starting point, then, is to share stories about church visits that were handled well and poorly, and how much it mattered to you to be received well.

The section that follows details best practices that healthy congregations employ. They require intentionality and some fresh thinking, but aren't costly or difficult.

Greet and get information on all visitors

Don't "pounce." First-time visitors typically prefer to observe, rather than to engage in energetic conversation. Pouncing conveys desperation. At the same time, visitors are sensitive about feeling ignored.

Friendly members are more effective than official "greeters" wearing official nametags. If members aren't instinctively friendly at this time, you can recruit and train greeters, but make sure they don't come across as just doing a Sunday job and thereby seeming insincere. Visitors are attentive to the quality of first greetings.

An attendance pad passed down each pew is an excellent way to capture name and e-mail address of visitors. Churches that don't have a history of using attendance pads need to start doing so. They are standard fare in most churches and aren't offensive to visitors.

Other than establishing a friendly tone, your primary goal is to secure the visitor's name and e-mail address. You might need to employ multiple tools for doing so: a pew attendance pad, a welcome packet in the back, greeters taking down names, a guest register, and a welcome table. Don't expect one method to do all of this critical work.

Capture Visitors' Names

Even though the typical church has multiple entry points, the most common tends to be Sunday worship. This can be an awkward but critical time for noticing visitors and capturing necessary information about them.

It is difficult to follow up with visitors if you don't know who they are or how to reach them. In this techno age, the most critical data is their name and their e-mail address.

Here's what you need to do:

- Evaluate your Sunday morning traffic flow. This is usually driven by architecture. Do you have multiple doors or a single door? Do visitors tend to come in by the main door? You want to position clergy at the most heavily used door, so that they can greet the visitor both before and after worship.

- Ask for their information. People aren't offended when you ask. It is standard practice. One method is for clergy and/or lay greeters to have information cards to hand each visitor. Guest registers tend to be less successful. Another method is a pew register that is handed down the pew at some point during the service. A backup procedure is to have a stack of visitor cards in a visible place. This is a backup plan, not a primary method.

- Don't introduce visitors during the service. That's premature and intrusive. It is, however, a good idea to use mid-service announcements to reinforce the importance of greeting and data-gathering. A church that is committed to growing its membership needs to be up-front and cheerful about the importance it places on meeting and following up with visitors.

Personal visit on day of first visit

A drop-by visit is best, with the expectation that a hello on the doorstep might be all that happens. The point is to acknowledge their visit and to communicate a desire to make their acquaintance.

The caller should have a leave-behind, such as a short, simple statement of welcome and what visitors mean to the congregation, not a lengthy description of the parish. Unless your pastor isn't skilled at calling, the first-Sunday caller should be a pastor. This establishes the priority that the congregation places on welcoming visitors and incorporating them into the community of faith. Freeing your pastor to make Sunday calls on visitors might require some fresh thinking about other Sunday duties, such as hospital visits and home communions. Sunday might be a day for trained laity to make such calls.

An exception to this practice of drop-by visits might be large cities, where people rarely expect to receive visitors in their apartments and would find an uninvited visitor strange.

Whatever method you employ, be sensitive to experience. Callers should note how they are received and should compare notes with other callers. Every context is different, but avoid anticipating a negative response to calling in order to avoid the awkwardness of making the call.

Send a brief, informative e-mail during first week

This message acknowledges the Sunday worship visit and contains links to the church web site, preferably to a special "visitors' spot" where the visitor can find information about the church, a schedule of upcoming events, an explanation of worship, an explanation of how people typically enter into the life of the community, and a Frequently Asked Questions section.

Have just one link in the welcome e-mail, rather than a long list of links, which could seem overwhelming. Get people to the web site, and let them explore at will.

Use a database-driven tracking process

A first visit should initiate a thorough process for leading the visitor from first-visit to affiliation.

Data should be gathered at every stage. You need to know where the obstacles are, where people tend to drop off. With this data, you can tweak the process constantly. For example, if you get good results on first few Sundays, but find that visitors don't respond to a newcomers class, you will want to evaluate that class: how invitations are sent, how often, with what tone, when class is offered, how class is perceived, whether class is even helpful.

After a newcomer's second visit to church:

- Send second e-mail, focus on an upcoming church event.
- Add visitor to e-mail newsletter distribution.
- Add visitor to special events invitation list, with focus on events that fit their perceived age or interest.

New Member Class

Offer a two-to-three-session class every one or two months. Use a tracking system to fine-tune frequency and content. Class should be part social, part listening; include food if possible. The focus should be on learning about the visitor, not selling the congregation or its denomination, and on responding to any preliminary questions they have.

If you offer instruction, it should be about faith questions, not denomination or congregation. People don't come to a church seeking an institution, but with yearnings and questions about faith. Don't stress parish history. That isn't likely to be a bridge-builder at this time. The pastor should be present, as important pastoral clues will come out in this class. Newcomers need to begin identifying the pastor as a spiritual leader.

Understand desired outcomes

The desired outcome for the church is to discern the personalities and needs of those whom God is bringing to this church. Each set of new members is a strong indicator of who the next set will be. The desired outcome for the visitor is to feel welcomed, informed, and invited. The desired outcome for parish leaders is to gather critical data on where the church needs to be going: what mission and ministry are indicated by member-ship trends? For example, a sudden influx of recently laid-off workers would suggest a ministry to workers in transition.

Provide regular opportunities to join

A New Member Class shouldn't be considered a requirement for membership. Avoid any appearance of legalism or of having to earn one's way in. Instead, provide a standard time in the Sunday service when people can make a decision to affiliate and come forward to be welcomed. Members need to see this happening all the time, not just a few times a year. Over time, adding members will seem normative, not threatening. If a new member hasn't attended the New Member Class, they can be invited to the class after joining. For congregations in which tradition requires a formal rite of joining, such as confirmation, a further incorporation offering can be instruction in that rite.

SUNDAY MORNING CHECKLIST FOR VISITORS

New members come to churches in many ways, but the most common by far is visiting on a Sunday morning. If you want your church to grow, you need to think through every detail of receiving visitors on Sunday.

Here is a checklist to guide your planning:

- Think through who will greet visitors before worship on Sunday.

    - The best greeter is the pastor. Leave the last-minute worship preparations to others. People remember churches where the pastor was out front greeting.

Continued

- Next best is a cadre of friendly ushers, who see their job as handshakes and smiles, not simply handing out a service bulletin.
- Both clergy and ushers should focus before-worship time on visitors, not on circling up with buddies. This might require teaching the congregation on why greeting visitors matters.

• Welcome Card

- Pastor should hand each visitor a 3 x 5 welcome card that asks for their name, e-mail address, and city (to identify tourists).
- Other information, such as their reason for visiting, should come out in a personal conversation.
- The key is e-mail address. With that, you can do extensive follow-up communications.
- Visitor should place welcome card in offering plate.

• After worship

- Visitors typically want to slip out unnoticed. There is little point in fighting that.
- Pastor should greet everyone at the door and make a point of thanking them for being part of the worshiping community today.
- Assign someone to collect welcome cards, look up telephone numbers and write them on the cards, and get the cards to the pastor right away.
- Pastor should try to telephone or call on every visitor that same afternoon. Keep the message simple: "glad you were here, would love to chat

Continued

further with you." If the visitor seems receptive, schedule a visit. If hesitant, say thanks and hope to see you next week.

- For the hesitant and for people not home, pastor should send a standard e-mail that afternoon, thanking them for being present and looking forward to seeing them again.

- First week

  - Welcome cards should go to whoever maintains parish data. Names and e-mail addresses should be entered. Start building a data file on each visitor, including date of visit, did pastor make contact, outcome of contact.

  - Add visitors to list for electronic newsletter. (See "Communications Strategy" for importance of switching to electronic communications.)

- Incorporation Process

  - Every congregation will handle this differently. The key is to have a process—classes, welcome dinners or lunches, handouts, new member celebrations—and to follow that process consistently with every visitor.

  - The ideal process will respond to the needs and interests of visitors, rather than to the institution's need to sell itself. How do you know what visitors' needs and interests are? You ask them. And you keep asking, and keep improving your process.

  - Remember: the typical visitor has no interest in helping your church to grow. They are consumers, and you need to know what they looking for.

NETWORK BUILDING

Decisions to visit and to join a congregation are complex processes. They happen differently for every person or family. The wise congregation offers many points at which a seeker can connect.

We now recognize that people exist in "networks," ranging from workgroups to social groups to interest groups. These networks enable like-minded people to find each other and to connect with each other in self-determining ways, often informal. The Internet is an example of a network.

Such networks tend to be "self-organizing," not formally structured or hierarchical. Faith communities work best when they function in this manner. They provide multiple points of connection—preschool, play group, day school, softball team, concerts, worship, support groups, and so on—and then put those in front of people in a way that facilitates engagement.

Networks are highly contextual and change constantly. The healthy church remains nimble in assessing how to connect with prospects and members. Methods evolve. The "test and measure" principle of Metrics applies. The softball team that engaged young adults one summer might not reach them at all a year later. Electronic tools like e-mail and a dynamic web site are perfect for encouraging networks. Static methods like permanent facilities and signboards tend to be ineffective.

Send Regular E-mails

They should be brief, focused, upbeat, and informative, each with an opportunity to engage (click on a link, sign up for an event, answer a survey, take a poll) and to unsubscribe. (See Chapter 3: Communications Strategy for best practices on content.) Each e-mail should have a specific focus, not be a grab-bag of invitations, appeals, and duty rosters. People will read short e-mails on a topic that interests them.

Be clear about how each mailing serves a primary parish purpose—group identity, for example. An acolyte duty roster should go only to acolytes and include a personal word from the acolyte master to the acolytes. Similarly, be sensitive to support needs. News about, say, a group for victims of abuse should go to members of that group, with a link to forward it to their friends, instead of being buried in a general mailing. Every mailing should keep in mind that you want recipients to forward these e-mails to friends. Thus, no "code lingo" that only parishioners would understand.

Draw People to Your Web Site

An effective web site is your primary window to the world. It will be the heart of networking, as people find connecti there, click to register for an event or to send e-mails to frie. and do some private exploring.

Thanks to web technology, your web site provides opportunities to track which pages visitors read and, therefore, where their interests lie. You get comparable insights from transaction pages (which events people register for or inquire about), downloadable files (such as sermons), and whether they use web tools to contact staff.

Instead of time-consuming and focus-losing announcements during Sunday worship, use e-mail and your web site to communicate positive values, such as transparency in operations, clarity in information, confidence in facts (not reliance on rumors), and leaders who are willing to be engaged.

Marketing

Church marketing needs to keep pace with marketing methods used by other ventures. The days of carefully honed mission statements, trifold brochures, and notices pinned on bulletin boards are over. (See Chapter 3: Communications Strategy for a complete presentation.)

People simply don't pay significant attention to postal mailing, especially to brochures and circulars. A short, visually interesting e-mail is more likely to be read.

Information, not salesmanship

In membership recruitment, helpful information matters more than salesmanship. Information should avoid in-house assumptions ("meeting at Barbara's house," with no further details), as well as code words and acronyms. Information to prospects and new members should go light on church politics. Prospects and new members aren't likely to value a church's institutional trials. Be clear about what is being offered and why (that is, benefit to be received).

Pay attention to image

Your goal is to establish a positive image. A congregation doesn't want to appear slick, but it does want to appear professional. Branding, copy, and editing should meet normal business standards. Remember: the competition for attention isn't between your marketing and another church's, but between your efforts and the many marketing appeals that prospects and new members receive from commerce and from other and usually better funded not-for-profits.

Your intended image needs to be about people and their ministries, not about facilities, denomination, or parish history.

Learn to harvest e-mail addresses

All e-mails should provide an opportunity to gather more e-mail addresses. All events should have a sign-in process that includes both name and e-mail address. Your web site should include a tool that enables member to update their own personal data, especially their e-mail address.

Use a professional e-mail handler (such as *www.aweber.com*) to make sure you verify permission to send and present a visible unsubscribe option. It is important to keep addresses up to date so that members neither miss out on things they are interested in nor become annoyed by unwanted e-mails.

SMALL GROUPS

Healthy congregations encourage members to form into small groups, also known as "cell groups" or what we call "circles of friends." These groups serve as the primary locus of belonging and peer-to-peer pastoral care. Because they don't depend on the direct participation of clergy or lay staff, they enable the congregation to be "scalable," that is, to grow far beyond the capacity of one or a few pastors to be primary caregivers.

In this section, we discuss some basic best practices for envisioning and getting started with small groups. A considerable body of study has arisen around small groups, in case you want to dig deeper. In fact, an Internet search on "small group ministry" will yield hundreds of websites devoted to detailed techniques for forming and nurturing small groups.

Basic Concepts of Small Groups

Healthy congregations focus membership development in small groups. Those groups can take many forms, but basically are small (eight to fifteen members) gatherings of people who agree to meet regularly (weekly, monthly) for the express purpose of forming Christian community. They can do work, pursue a spiritual or study agenda, or meet for social enjoyment. The point is the gathering and the trusting and loving relationships that emerge over time. In a healthy congregation, this small group is the setting for belonging and care-giving to take place. Some pastoral emergencies, like hospitalization or death, require the congregation's pastoral staff to respond as well.

In a healthy congregation, new groups are constantly being formed and new members, as well as longtime members, are being encouraged to join them. The idea of focusing a parish's membership ministries in small groups will seem old hat to many church leaders and far-fetched, even threatening, to others. The main rationale for small groups within the church is simple, though: small groups were the model for Jesus' ministry.

Jesus was surrounded by hierarchical models of organization, from imperial army and courts to Jewish temple cult to patriarchal family. Instead of adopting any of these, Jesus formed circles of friends, in which providing care for people and support during times of trouble mattered far more than allocating power.

These were "flat" organizations, to use a modern term, meaning they were inclusive of all, self-regulating, non-hierarchical, not concerned with wealth or power, not directly tied to his charisma. The tight command-and-control model that Christianity later adopted was a creation of the early Church, not a model established by Jesus. The circles formed by Jesus focused on transformation of life, healing, learning about the in-breaking Kingdom of God, and serving others. The first apostles added table fellowship and communal property. They existed as long as they were needed and effective, not forever as immutable tradition or local custom.

Primary Purposes of Small Groups

To justify the hard work that is required to establish and maintain small groups, and to trust their inevitable impact on the congregation, it is important to understand the purposes that small groups serve.

Face-to-face interaction

For Jesus, the principle governing all relationships was love. That love was personal—person forgiving person, enemies reconciling, neighbors providing succor, parents and children finding oneness. Out of that love, people served and sacrificed.

In our relatively anonymous society, with "virtual relationships" often substituting for personal interaction, the Christian small group serves a vital purpose that is somewhat new to religious life, namely, enabling people to have non-competitive and value-centered face-to-face interaction.

Locus of belonging within the larger body

Jesus didn't live to see the day of a large fellowship. Other than two mass feedings, his time was spent with a small entourage (twelve named male disciples, several named female disciples, and several dozen others) who traveled about with him and occasionally went out to serve. Their lives together appear to have been informal and not governed by any agenda or timetable. Jesus went where he went, and they went with him.

The Twelve had a special relationship with each other, as did other men and women following Jesus. They were a model, or paradigm, of what Jesus envisioned for all of his followers. The point wasn't their unique or elite status, but what they gave up in order to follow Jesus, namely, careers, families, homes, wealth, and safety. In the days after Pentecost, the apostles tried to maintain this way of being: meeting in homes, sharing property, and focusing on being together and worshiping God.

Helping members learn to live in community

To speak in generalizations—to which there are always exceptions—modern American adults have little community in their lives. Other than workgroups—a shifting population, often competitive—and nuclear family, they rarely spend significant time with other people. Their relationships tend to be functional, not personal; episodic, not continuous; and to have self-defined and largely self-serving purposes.

Christian community offers a potent answer to this lack of community. But it will need to be learned, almost from scratch. Small groups are the setting where people will learn basic lessons, such as:

- how to interact frequently and continuously with people other than family
- how to adapt to group norms and purposes without sacrificing personal integrity
- how to listen to other people and to share oneself
- how to compromise, to resolve conflict, to reach consensus
- how to value being, as well as doing
- and self-sacrificial love, as well as role-defined function.

Giving and receiving care

As stoic as we are about getting along alone, we ache for the care that can only be given by another person. Our marriages and partnerships cannot bear the full burden of providing such care. We wear each other out. In a Christian small group, participants can tell their stories, share their aspirations and fears, seek specific help in crises, and relax into the unqualified love of people who are just glad to see them.

Even more than receiving such care is the joy of giving it. Dying to self truly is our pathway to life.

Seeing God at work

It is one thing to confess Jesus as Lord and to accept his statement that "God is love." It is quite another to see that Lordship and love actually happening in one's presence. It's the foundational principle of an incarnational faith. God is a being who can be seen and known, perhaps imperfectly and yet sufficiently to warrant devotion.

A small Christian group is a place where one takes the risk of living as Jesus wanted us to live and, in the process, sees the one whom Jesus called "Father."

Daring transformation of life

Jesus said that God was "making all things new." Eventually, that becomes personal: one's own life is being transformed.

Our resistance to such transformation is substantial:

- fear of losing face or being judged wrong
- loss of status, privilege
- loss of certainties that have led one to feel safe
- need to examine one's life and to accept responsibility for expressions of will
- need to accept one's flaws, limitations, and failures.

In most settings of our lives, the cost of transformation is too high. Small groups provide a safe, accepting, non-judgmental, and intimate place where the risks can be undertaken.

Operating Principles of Small Groups

Small groups function most effectively when allowed the freedom to function as members desire. That doesn't mean "anything goes," for healthy groups need to have certain norms and accountability to the larger congregation. Rather than insist on uniformity in how groups function, the best practice is to monitor groups' behavior, to intervene when people are getting hurt, and to celebrate diversity.

Here are some basic operating principles as a guide for getting started with small groups:

Size and frequency

* Optimal size is eight to fifteen participants
* Leave room for members to bring friends
* When regular attendance exceeds fifteen, form a new group
* Optimal frequency is no less than monthly, preferably more often.

Leadership

Each group should be facilitated by a trained and accountable leader, who has been approved by pastoral staff. This isn't for purposes of control, but to verify maturity, suitability for such a task, and availability for the necessary time commitment. Direct involvement of pastoral staff in selecting, training, and supporting group leaders affirms small groups as a key component of the overall work of the congregation, and not a rogue movement.

Training should include basic instruction on:

* group dynamics
* listening
* setting and observing group norms
* accountability.

Purpose

In its identity, activities, and purposes, each group will reflect the needs and personalities of its original members. As those needs change, as personal development occurs and new faces emerge, the group will need to evolve. This can be difficult for founding members to accomplish. When a group reaches a certain threshold of transformation, it might need to dissolve so that new groups can emerge.

In training group leaders, pastoral staff need to equip them to recognize such evolving realities, to deal with inevitable conflict, and to recognize the need to re-form.

GROUP NORMS INCLUDE:

- confidentiality
- regular participation
- openness, transparency
- listening
- keeping group life in the group
- avoiding temptation to "fix" another group member.

SCENARIOS TO ANTICIPATE AND BE PREPARED FOR INCLUDE:

- conflict
- manipulative behavior, passive-aggression
- unfair sharing of "air-time"
- fixing and amateur therapy
- breach of confidentiality
- pressure to have all groups be alike.

Accountability

Facilitators are accountable to professional staff. This isn't a control mechanism, but a process for building a healthy partnership. Group leaders should refer in-depth needs to pastoral staff.

Groups will need to make decisions about where they fall on spectra such as social, prayer, study, activity, and mission work. New groups should form regularly, to incorporate new or not-yet-participating members and their friends. Group members will need to be reminded that cliquishness reveals a lack of trust in God's desire for inclusion and love.

The Goal is Transformation, not Perfection

Among the "tapes" that we learn in childhood and need to unlearn as adults is a belief that God expects perfection and that the goal of religious life is to attain perfection. In teaching the classic spiritual disciplines—such as prayer, worship, confession—we need to convey another message, namely, that God wants transformation of life, not a finished state called Perfection. Faith is a journey, not an arrival and then a stopping.

In teaching prayer, for example, we teach people how to talk with God, how to open themselves to the holy, and how to sit in silence before God. The aim of prayer is an awareness of God's presence, not perfect wording, posture or attitude. Similarly, in teaching the discipline of fasting—an often overlooked but, in my opinion, essential spiritual discipline—the goal isn't an approved protocol for giving up food, but an emptying of self so that God can fill. By avoiding any suggestion of perfection, the one fasting won't be surprised when the consequences of fasting are emotional vulnerability and a certain confusion.

Perhaps the hardest place to let go of perfection is worship. Church leaders tend to work hard at the "performance" side of worship, with practices for key participants, evaluations, and careful planning. Such efforts can be a sign of taking worship seriously, but they shouldn't be allowed to promote a perfectionism that leaves no room for the accidental or personal, like a burst of laughter, an onset of weeping, or a child's playfulness. Perfectionist worship tends to become stiff and stilted.

Transformation, by contrast, is inherently chaotic and messy. It follows no single path. As a preacher I know said recently, it usually involves two steps forward and one step back. Look at how wild the ride was for Jesus' disciples. By focusing on transformation, the church's spiritual guidance becomes liberating and encouraging, not confining and hyper-parental.

CHAPTER

Leadership Development

EFFECTIVE LEADERSHIP is critical to any enterprise, including the faith community. It is essential that the congregation work at recruiting, preparing, and supporting effective leaders who can implement "best practices" and nurture wellness.

In a healthy system, leaders are recruited, trained, supported, and held accountable. Those who aspire to leadership are screened, not simply handed the reins of authority. Training doesn't seek to perpetuate the status quo, but rather to affirm identity and values and to nurture healthy norms, such as welcoming change.

CHALLENGE FOR CHURCHES

Leadership might be the greatest challenge facing churches. Churches tend to treat good leadership as an accident, not as a requirement that they work hard to achieve. By not saying no to unqualified persons who present themselves for leadership, congregations risk hurting morale among capable leaders, as well as suboptimal performance. By not recruiting leaders, churches encourage self-replicating and closed leadership circles, which lead, in turn, to stale ideas and resistance to change.

Moreover, by removing clergy from the leadership recruitment and training processes, churches encourage an antagonism-based view of lay leadership—"our job is to keep the clergy in line"—and they disempower the one person who tends to know all members, including newcomers, and to have a broad perspective on congregational needs.

Some better ways to organize lay-leaders:

- Engage clergy directly in the leadership development process, with a direct role in identifying promising leaders, recruiting them, and training them.

- Require all leaders to participate in training programs that are appropriate to their duties and to their level of responsibility.

- Hold leaders accountable for performance of their duties, according to agreed-upon standards.

- Ground leaders in an awareness that, for a church, transformation of persons matters more than continuity of institution, and that change and conflict aren't mistakes to be avoided, but necessary attributes of health.

- Seek leaders who function effectively in non-hierarchical systems, in which autonomy and individual creativity are valued more than conservation, where leaders give permission and preserve freedom rather than exercise control.

Cautions

Efforts to improve leadership structures and expectations will provoke stiff resistance. Many people keep God "small" by keeping their clergy small. They avoid a deep and life-transforming encounter with God by keeping their churches off-balance. They avoid Jesus' teachings on wealth and power by fighting over wealth and power. Dysfunctional systems work hard to preserve their dysfunctional behaviors and to punish those who promote health. They resist change and encourage weak leadership.

In many churches, clergy are isolated. Any move to end that isolation—by encouraging clergy-lay partnership, or by involving clergy in recruiting lay leaders—will be perceived as threatening. Many laity, especially long-time members, view leadership as an entitlement, not as a ministry to which certain persons are called.

These are systemic issues of long standing. They can be changed, but only with a significant commitment to seeking best practices and to letting go of self-destructive ways. Healthy leadership will require a commitment to openness, accountability, network-building, and lay-clergy partnering that will be new to most congregations and profoundly disturbing to some. It will be work for the entire congregation, not a process where a few go to a leadership seminar and then try to pass on fresh ideas.

BASIC CONCEPTS:

1. Network-based, non-hierarchical, leadership

Healthy organizations are "flattening" the org chart to encourage teamwork, free-flowing relationships, and individual creativity. Even traditionally pyramidal organizations like the military and corporations find that teams perform well when allowed freedom in decision-making and responding to changed circumstances.

This is new behavior requires new attitudes toward power, control, and accountability, as well as

Continued

heightened trust in people to function responsibly outside command-and-control structures.

Basic principles (as outlined by Fred Burnham, of the Institute for Servant Leadership, in his paper "Network Theory & Church Leadership"):

A healthy church needs to show **"environmental sensitivity,"** that is, an ability to identify contextual changes promptly and to respond to them. A hierarchical or bureaucratic structure discourages such sensitivity by its tendency to assign blame, rather than learn from the unexpected; by self-protective behavior at every level; and by slowness of response. Teams and individuals "close to the ground" see more and respond better.

A healthy church avoids "centralized control," because centralized control slows communication, discourages the taking of initiative, and hampers healthy relationships. Instead, the healthy church encourages an **open system**, in which information and ideas flow freely and rapidly and people organize themselves to deal with needs.

A healthy church values "individual agency," that is, individuals functioning beyond rules and boundaries to do what they do well.

A healthy church encourages **"self-organization,"** in which "enterprising individuals begin to select gifted teammates to work with them," Burnham writes.

Open and transparent communication, which Burnham calls "Scale-Free Communication," generates

Continued

more and better information, enables the network to adapt effectively, and avoids secrets or "in-crowd" knowledge.

Even though homogeneity might feel more comfortable, "**Diversity**" yields richer information and problem-solving. Leadership circles must mirror the diversity of the larger congregation.

A healthy church values "**Innovation and Adaptation**," as opposed to resisting change.

2. **Leaders understand and value network-based leadership**

As they envision and carry out their work in church, effective leaders will resist the tendency to emulate hierarchies they know at work or prior church experience. Instead, starting with the leadership cadre itself, they will model open, free-flowing, decentralized, and spontaneous functioning.

A critical starting point will be transparency and abundant information. Leaders will tell others what they are doing, will share information widely, even negative news, and will encourage feedback.

Leaders will listen to groups and individuals, rather than tell them what to do. Leaders will identify problems rather than compel specific solutions.

Leaders will maintain appropriate boundaries and not fill every vacuum.

Leaders will self-regulate to discourage "take-charge" behavior, whether born of frustration or enthusiasm or a need for control.

Continued

3. **Leaders see their roles as network-support, not running things**

   Jesus formed circles of friends, not a hierarchical institution concerned with allocating power.

   Jesus saw leaders as servants, nurturing those circles, not as managers running an institution.

   Whether circles form intentionally or spontaneously, they benefit from an environment of freedom and healthy norms. Leaders establish and protect that environment and affirm healthy norms. For example:

   - Networks depend on effective tools of communications, not facilities. Leaders will affirm a norm of open flows of information, and will provide open access to communication tools.

   - To promote diversity and self-organization, leaders will establish a norm of inclusiveness and will monitor networks for signs of closed doors.

   - Leaders will monitor formation of groups and, if necessary, will assist in their formation, so that members unaccustomed to network-based participation can learn to trust it and function effectively in it.

Leaders Need Training for the Church Context

In some ways, churches are like other institutions:

- Like a business, they deal with property, budget, personnel, and customer service.
- Like a school, they deal with knowledge, teaching, and curricula.

- Like a social set, they deal with belonging, volunteering, manners, and privilege.

- Like a family, they deal with emotions, deep connectedness, and continuity.

Leaders in these other institutions often assume that their leadership skills are transferable to church. However, they don't question how effectively their organizations function, and what new leadership skills would be required if they were to function more effectively. They rarely do deep analysis of their organization, except to study short-term ways to maximize profits, increase enrollments, or reduce conflict.

The one exception are entrepreneurs, who are constantly reinventing their businesses and their roles in them. They are highly motivated to analyze and to change. Some of the most pertinent reading for church systems is coming out of the entrepreneurial world, especially the Internet and franchising. Books like *The E-Myth Revisited* (Michael Gerber), *Creating Customer Evangelists* (Ben McConnell and Jackie Huba), and *Permission Marketing* (Seth Godin) are highly relevant.

In two ways, therefore, the church suffers from this assumption of transferable leadership skills:

The church is unique and requires unique leadership skills—skills that sometimes are exactly the opposite of what a business or university needs. Risk management, for example, is valued in most secular organizations. In a faith community, however, risks such as new ideas, new patterns of relationships, and new ministries need room to flourish, even to crash and burn.

On top of all this, churches are changing:

- Some are in various stages of decline, ranging from gradual loss of membership to severe shrinkage.

- Some are growing and feeling new pressures on space, staff, ministry focus, and familiarity.

- Some face changes in their immediate context and are having to decide whether to adapt.
- Some see new constituencies changing the shape of the fellowship.
- Some feel a need to serve people in different ways or to have a different role in the larger community.
- Some, in response to changing political and economic forces, find that business-as-usual no longer seems adequate.

Understand the Fundamentals of Church Leadership

Church leadership is unique

Ways in which church leadership differs from other types of leadership include:

- less need for managing, more for nurturing
- accepts failure (a better teacher than success)
- concerned with servanthood, not advancement
- seeks transformation, not comfort
- seeks renewal, not continuity
- seeks repentance (change of mind), not status quo
- encourages freedom, discourages control
- defends the weak, rather than reward the strong
- forms circles of friendship, not hierarchies of power
- values self-organizing networks, rather than directed systems
- embraces risk, rather than avoiding or managing risk.

Church leaders are unique

Church leaders are different from leaders in other organizations in that they are:

- collaborators, not competitors
- liberators, not controllers
- listeners, not order-givers
- team-builders, not power-brokers
- assertive, but not arrogant
- visionary, but able to bend
- concerned with transformation of persons, not institutional maintenance
- story-tellers, not dogmatists.

Recruiting Leaders

Churches must be intentional, not casual, about selecting both lay and clergy leaders.

Probe deeply

- Interview prospective leaders (especially on prior experiences in leadership, reasons for being available for leadership now, expectations of fellow leaders, and self-perceived strengths and weaknesses as a leader).
- Assess their leadership characteristics.
- Seek their vision for the church's future.
- Assess their willingness to take risks, make changes, and see freshly.
- Interview those who work with them.
- Evaluate communications skills and transparency.
- Remember that those who are controlling or resistant to change or risk at work are likely to bring these characteristics to their church position.

Assess prospective leaders' previous performance in church leadership

- Trusted and respected leaders are likely to be trustworthy again.
- Troublemakers and dividers aren't likely to change.
- Maintain a confidential file on assessments of leaders' performance.
- Character matters more than specific skills.
- Getting free legal advice or accounting skills or web support doesn't begin to outweigh the damage that can be done by a leader with poor character.
- You can hire specialists for specific tasks; you can't hire character.

Select the Best

- Don't hesitate to say no to an unqualified leader.
- If a prospect's ego or loyalty depends on being selected for a leadership post, he or she isn't a good candidate.
- No one has "earned the right" to church leadership.
- Fresh eyes will see more than jaded eyes, but experience has its own value. The age of a candidate is no predictor of his or her abilities.
- Diversity is important, because every constituency in the membership needs to see his or her "face" reflected in leadership ranks.
- Balance is important, so that all ideas get a fair hearing.
- Social prominence and business prominence count for little in the church's unique requirements.

BRIDGING THE CLERGY-LAY LEADERSHIP GAP

A typical congregation has no end of complex relationships. Folks, after all, are folks. But the most complex of all might be the relationship between the pastor and the top lay leader. Lay leaders aren't a countervailing force to keep the clergy in line; they are colleagues in a shared task. Clergy need to be consulted in selecting lay leaders.

Sometimes, the relationship is smooth and serene, as well as fruitful. More often, though, the relationship ranges from awkward to strained to radioactive. Why? Personality conflicts happen, but the usual cause of strain is deeper: each wants to run the congregation, and, more often than not, each is convinced that he or she can do a better job than the other.

Rarely is this articulated or addressed. It just sits there, sometimes simmering and boiling over, sometimes erupting in leadership meetings, sometimes bearing acidic fruit in a patronizing attitude in one-on-one meetings. To some extent, this is just politics: two strong-willed people who want to get their way. But it goes deeper. Down deep, each believes that he or she has the best interests of the parishioners at heart and is protecting the flock from the other.

Sometimes the conflict zeroes in on money, because money is readily understood. The pastor wants to spend money, the lay leader wants to conserve it. Or the pastor wants to pursue the bold and innovative, the lay leader wants to "do the basics" first. Or the pastor wants to take risks in deficit budgeting, the lay leader considers that foolish. The issue, of course, isn't money—it's control, vision, and attitudes toward risk. Those are hard to discuss; it's easier to get feisty about the budget.

Sometimes the conflict focuses on worship. The pastor considers that to be his or her bailiwick, and the lay leader gets tired of Sunday afternoon complaints. The pastor wants to be spontaneous in responding to the unexpected need, the lay leader wants to soothe parishioners with stable and predictable ministries. The pastor wants to keep a prickly music minister happy by approving challenging but unpopular music, the lay leader cannot fathom offering music no one wants to sing. The roles can be reversed, with the lay leader wanting more innovation and responsiveness than the pastor wants. The issue, of course, isn't worship. It's still about control, vision, and change. And these subjects are still hard to talk about.

Here are some best practices for dealing with these issues (success isn't guaranteed!):

- Name the issue: don't make money or worship or some beloved parishioner a scapegoat. Talk about what really should be on table.

- Talk directly: don't triangulate by talking through a third party, or seeking alliances. Your most important ministry as leaders is to make your relationship work. The parish cannot be healthier than your direct relationship.

- Listen deeply: to resolve anything, you must understand and respect each other. To do that, you must know each other.

- Ask for help: not through triangulation, but through mediation, coaching, or counseling. When you are at odds, the congregation knows it and are waiting to see how you resolve matters. You become the model for other disputes. Be a good model.

These best practices won't necessarily work. Folks, as I say, are folks, and ingenious in defying common sense. But we have an obligation to try. The entire system depends on it.

TRAINING LEADERS

All designated leaders need training, not just the central few, so that all can share common values, understand emerging visions, and trust each other. Clergy need to be involved, although not necessarily as lead trainers. One way to break down distrust between clergy and laity is to encourage them to work together as trustworthy colleagues. Another way is to give each a stake in the other's effective performance.

Foundational Skills

Skills required of church leaders include:

* basic Bible knowledge
* principles of servant leadership
* understanding of church organizational issues and opportunities.

Theology of Christian leadership

The biblical model encourages us to strive for church leadership that is:

* non-hierarchical
* relational, not power-based
* set apart
* forward-thinking
* pastoral
* education focused
* encouraging of mercy, generosity, inclusion, love, transformation, and spiritual formation.

Family Systems Theory

All families tend to develop unique systems for:

- integrating family members
- making decisions
- allocating resources
- using time
- setting priorities
- resolving conflict.

Certain archetypes tend to recur:

- single-authority (patriarchal, matriarchal, single-parent)
- shared parental authority (partners as a team)
- shared authority (parents and children, especially older children)
- function-based authority (e.g. one parent makes financial decisions, another makes child-care decisions)
- leaderless.

Functional families show certain characteristics

- All are included.
- All are valued.
- All are heard.
- Roles are clearly understood and flexible.
- Behavior has consequences.
- Rules, boundaries, and norms are understood.

Dysfunctional families show different characteristics:

- Inclusion is conditional, inconsistent, used as a weapon to compel compliance or to punish.
- Not all needs matter.

- Family members are assigned roles, not of their choosing, such as:
  - ○ scapegoat
  - ○ rebel
  - ○ hero
  - ○ caretaker.
- Members guess at what is normal.
- No one tells the whole truth; instead, innuendo, conspiracy, and manipulation are preferred.
- Chaos reigns.
- Consequences are inconsistent, often disproportionate.
- Norms and rules change by whim.
- System often exists to feed one member's addiction (father's alcoholism, mother's drug addiction, child's anorexia or self-destructive impulses).

Churches tend to behave like family systems. It's the human-to-human system that we know best. We tend to replicate the system of our family of origin, because we know how to play by those rules. Unless wise and assertive leaders intervene, a church system will tend to be a compendium, and collision, of different family-system styles and expectations.

Some will see the pastor as a partner with certain roles to perform. Some will see the pastor as a parent figure and therefore as a danger, caregiver, obstacle to self-gratification, tyrant, or whatever they knew as a child. Some will see the pastor as a child, to be trivialized and controlled.

Church members can fall into roles such as scapegoat or hero. Certain members will want to be the pastor's "co-parent" in managing the "children," even to the point of intimacy.

Members will "partner up" to seize control of the family. Some will find in this partnership the intimacy they lack at home. Members will take sides against each other. Older members, for example, will claim the privileges of seniority, while younger members will play on their energy and children's needs. The well-to-do will freeze out the have-nots, and the have-nots, if mobilized, will return the favor. Arguments will arise about other people's morality, life choices, sexuality, and beliefs—all the while avoiding self-examination and repentance.

Leaders need to understand such dynamics if they are to handle information (formal and informal, statistics and rumors, praise and complaint) and make appropriate responses to outcomes. Leaders need to set a good standard in how they manage their own life as a leadership cadre. If the leadership circle is dysfunctional, the whole system will become unhealthy.

A critical relationship is the partnership between clergy and key lay leaders. In dealing with a dysfunctional system, this relationship is the place to start working for health. As in a family, it is difficult for the group as a whole to be any healthier than the relationships between the leaders.

Life-cycles

All living systems go through predictable life cycles:

- birth
- formation (adolescence)
- maturity
- decline
- death.

Healthy systems work to avoid decline and death by using the calm of maturity to plan a rebirth. That seems counterintuitive, to be planning the new even as the current has abundant signs of life, and it often frustrates people who are finally getting to enjoy the fruits of maturity. Nevertheless, failure to anticipate the future will guarantee even greater frustration and conflict during decline, all at a time of reduced financial vitality.

Unhealthy systems avoid change as long as possible, often until death is staring them in the face. They use the decline stage to blame persons or groups for causing the decline, thereby damaging trust and community. They squander limited resources in trying to stave off death. They avoid critical self-examination and therefore enter into reduce-the-pain efforts with little knowledge of context or opportunity. They just want the pain of dying to stop.

Assessing a system's current life-cycle stage isn't easy. It depends on metrics (quantitative measures), more than on feelings of satisfaction or absence of conflict. It requires more candor about vitality and momentum than custodians of present activities are likely to welcome.

Leaders need to step back from a role they often take, namely being agents for church members in promoting members' immediate interests. Their other role is to be custodians of the system, like parents or a board of directors, anticipating the future even as others enjoy the present. If decline has begun and the air is filled with blame and frustration, leaders need to become analytical and calm, not partisans for one source of blaming or another.

Some members, and leaders, will use decline or death to pursue a personal agenda—like getting rid of the pastor, stopping a certain ministry, or reining in mission—even though that agenda has nothing to do with causes of decline or the pathway to renewed health. In a healthy system, key leaders will resist being sucked into such agendas.

As with the development of a human person, each life-cycle stage requires certain leadership activities.

During **birth or rebirth**, leaders need to:

- encourage risk-taking (like learning to walk)
- protect new ideas and new constituencies from attack (by change-resisters, for example)
- provide appropriate "discipline" to those whose enthusiasm blinds them to outcomes or to their impact on the overall system
- move from hand-holding to giving wings, as new ideas, new ministries, and new constituencies are "pushed from the nest" to fly on their own.

During **formation**, leaders need to:

- exercise patience as groups and persons want more autonomy than they are prepared to handle
- work as a unit (like united parents) to give a consistent message and to maintain a focus on the overall system
- encourage risk-taking and learning from failure
- invest in change
- protect risk-takers from attack by opponents sensing an opportunity to pounce.

During **maturity**, leaders need to:

- start the process of self-examination and needs analysis that will lead to strategies for averting decline and death
- keep the system open
- encourage "pioneers" to keep imagining as "settlers" enjoy the moment
- set aside resources for strategies leading to rebirth (e.g. adding space, adding staff, developing a new-ministries fund).

If **decline** cannot be averted, leaders need to:

- use decline as a time to reassess long-term objectives
- use decline to contemplate options for revitalization (rebirth)
- estimate costs (financial, human) of revitalization
- do a sober assessment of whether such costs can be handled
- if so, how will resources be assembled and deployed?
- if not, how will leaders prepare for a gracious death?

This is extraordinarily hard work, requiring discernment and oneness in leadership ranks at precisely the time when leaders feel pulled in opposite directions, both by their own interests and by the tug of parishioners. To do this work effectively, leaders will need to stand apart from the membership, not to isolate themselves from conflicting pressures, but to gain perspective that rises above emotions.

Even as members look for whom to blame (often targeting the clergy), leaders will need to work in partnership with the clergy and understand that a congregation's decline usually has roots that precede current lay or clergy leaders.

If **death** is the end, then leaders need to:

- be bold and faithful in facing death
- make generous disposition of assets, in partnership with judicatory and community
- remind members that, as Christians, we don't fear death
- remind members that all institutions eventually outlive their original charter and either change radically or die
- declare that a gracious death can be a sign of God's love
- believe that, in God's realm, the death of a specific institution won't be the end of God's concern for its members or its context; something new and good will be born
- remind members that death is a sign of life, not of failure.

Dysfunctional Systems: Causes and Correction

Human systems can become dysfunctional: trapped in hurtful behaviors, spiraling from one failure to another, unable to make the wise decisions or course corrections that would end the spiral.

What is a "dysfunctional church"?

Dysfunction doesn't mean decline, organizational problems, budget shortfalls, membership losses, or failure in mission. Those are normal, if regrettable, conditions in which any system can find itself. Dysfunction means impaired, abnormal, or unhealthy conditions, usually in interpersonal relations, which result in:

- hurting other people
- making consistently poor decisions
- engaging in self-defeating behaviors, such as
    - sexual misconduct
    - addictions
    - unethical choices
    - scapegoating of the vulnerable
    - deceitful rumoring.

In a dysfunctional church, as in a dysfunctional family, people seem isolated, afraid of each other, confused, unable to trust, depressive.

What causes a church to become "dysfunctional"?

One cause is a trauma such as sexual misconduct or addiction in key leaders, which was hidden, allowed to continue too long, and not addressed openly. A healthy system can weather any storm, including such violations as sexual misconduct by a pastor or key lay leader. An unhealthy system goes into shock, denial, depression, and eventually dysfunction, that is, an inability to function effectively.

In some cases, the cause is a drastic change in conditions, such as a natural disaster or economic dislocation, which wasn't addressed as a problem requiring action by the community, but was used as an occasion to blame a despised minority, to scapegoat the vulnerable, or to gain narrow advantage, and the community allowed this lie to proceed. Another possible cause is the emotional, mental, or moral collapse of a key leader, which wasn't handled with compassion toward the individual and fresh direction for the system, but was hidden, denied, defended, rejected as unworthy of concern, or made to seem a normative part of the system's life.

Like a virus, the dysfunctional element in the church tends to replicate itself and undermine treatment efforts.

Newcomers sense the dysfunction, although they rarely can name it, and they flee. The outsider's perspective that is so critical to seeing dysfunction ceases to occur.

Leaders who have learned to live with the dysfunction and to benefit from it (called "enablers" in addiction), tend to assume positions of power. To defend their hold on power, they tend to resist healing.

What can be done about a dysfunctional church?

Healing a dysfunctional church is difficult work, and often cannot be accomplished.

Most clergy aren't trained adequately for leading such a recovery effort. Few laity have the time, skill, or emotional energy to engage in long-term healing. Outside help will be needed, and a considerable investment of money and time. Even with professional help, the dysfunctional system might resist all corrective efforts and need to die so that something new can be born.

Leaders have difficult and self-effacing roles to play. For one thing, current leaders could be part of the problem, that is, directly causing the conditions that sustain dysfunction. Most likely, if they can be led to recognize their enabling, they will need to resign. Fresh leaders will be needed, who are less tinged by participation in dysfunctional behaviors and decisions, and more able to see the system as it is.

Leaders will need to accept the necessity of investing in outside resources. Sick systems don't get well without significant help. Leaders will need to break free from any culture of denial and hiding. This will be a time for radical transparency, even at the risk of embarrassing certain leaders and members. Legal assistance might be helpful in determining how to handle certain matters, but a lawyer's natural tendency to control information and to say as little as possible should be resisted. For trust and confidence to be restored, people need to know and to talk.

If it seems likely that the system will need to die in order to be reborn, leaders will have the cheerless task of protecting assets, working with the judicatory on issues of property ownership and continuity of mission.

Conflict Management

Conflicts are a constant in church life. For example, conflicts may exist:

- between clergy and lay leaders
- among members of a staff
- between ministry leaders and participants (e.g. choir director and choir)
- among age groups
- between men and women
- between long-tenure and short-tenure
- between liberals and conservatives.

Just listing some of the possibilities suggests a fundamental truth: a living system will have conflict. The leadership issue isn't whether conflict will occur, but how to handle the many conflicts that are occurring at any given time.

In general, a healthy church system can handle even severe conflicts. The best long-term strategy for dealing with conflicts isn't to stifle disagreement, to rein in strong personalities, or to avoid situations that are likely to produce conflict (such as change, politics, or financial problems). The best strategy is to nurture a healthy church.

When conflicts arise, therefore, the leadership need isn't to assign blame or to minimize fallout. The need is to assess the system's state of wellness. Is the system healthy enough to handle this latest conflict? The leaders' focus is church wellness, not preventing conflict or taking sides in a conflict. The primary exception—and it happens frequently—is leadership conflict involving the pastor.

Any conflict involving the clergy evokes complex responses, such as:

- odd and often childish behaviors among laity
- feelings of guilt and powerlessness
- a rekindling of issues from childhood
- denial during early stages, when resolution is most possible, and then bursts of rage
- a tendency to load onto this one target a host of issues that have little to do with the specifics of the presenting problem
- a pathological desire for secrecy
- an antagonist who is determined to unseat the pastor and will do anything to make that happen.

Leadership groups have difficulty handling such a conflict. Their ranks usually include both those most critical of the pastor and those most supportive. Norms such as consensus, civility, open discussion, and patience tend to evaporate.

Lay leaders tend to stop seeing their role as working in partnership with the clergy and to start seeing it as being advocates for the laity against the pastor. Being an advocate can include steps toward resolution and peace, but always with an air of suspicion and confrontation.

Leaders become overwhelmed with data input—complaints, rumors, innuendo, love stories, horror stories, suggestions, threats—coming in broadside fashion from the laity, like undifferentiated noise, and in tightly focused anguish from the clergy, and leaders are increasingly expected to take sides. If the leadership conflict goes from simmering to boiling, leaders will be expected to punish and hurt someone. They become seen as "enforcers."

Fortunately, an entire industry of church conflict-resolution specialists has arisen, making expertise and proven processes available to the congregation. Unfortunately, those services are expensive, begin to consume leaders' time, and usually lead to the pastor's resignation, as this is easier than trying to change the attitudes and behaviors of a large group.

Even more unfortunately, the conditions that led to the clergy-leadership conflict rarely are resolved by "fixing" or "ousting" the pastor. They are systemic issues, and they don't go away easily. For that reason, the leadership might come to a resolution of a clergy-employment issue, but find that nothing has improved.

From a leadership training perspective, the primary need is to understand these dynamics and not to be surprised or ashamed when they occur.

SUPPORTING LEADERS

Leaders aren't "wind-up machines" that you wind up once and start in motion. They are persons with needs, distractions, frailties, and blind sides, as well as capabilities to be honored and nurtured.

Monitor leaders' performance, because

- a frustrated leader can become destructive
- a destructive leader can frustrate many others
- an effective leader needs to be recognized and tagged for future duties
- unresolved conflict within a task group or ministry group can spill over into general congregational life.

Hold leaders accountable: it shows them that their work matters. Examples:

- Take attendance at leadership meetings.
- Set a policy specifying consequences for missing meetings, and then enforce it.
- Resist secrecy; instead publish leadership outcomes, including comments.
- Take action when a leader behaves in a destructive way.
- Track fulfillment of assignments.

Provide "care and feeding." Leaders need pastoral care if they are to provide care to others. Church leaders don't expect payment, but they do expect to be recognized and thanked.

Opportunities for continuing education for leaders not only enhance their skills, but show respect. "Trickle-down inspiration" events tend to have less impact than skill enhancements. For example, instead of sending a leader to a seminar on the importance of managing conflict, send them to a local business school or counseling agency for skills training in how to manage conflict. Don't expect a leader to attend an event and then come back to "light a fire," unless you have also prepared the congregation for accepting fresh vision or ideas.

One critical gift to lay leaders is spiritual direction by the clergy. When a pastor provides spiritual direction to leaders, it establishes a healthy relationship between pastor and member, and it takes the leader deeper into what they have to offer as a leader and why they offer it.

Don't abuse willingness by assigning too many duties. When a willing leader has too many duties, he or she tends to be less effective in all of them, burn out is likely to occur, and others are denied an opportunity to serve. Better to let a program die than to stretch a leader too thin. Leaders need to be spared the misapprehension that they are indispensable and that they "own" certain activities or groups

Avoid Discouraging Lay Ministers

Here are three guaranteed ways to discourage lay ministers:

1. Give them an assignment, and then take it back because they aren't doing it your way or because you are anxious.
2. Ignore their work, as if it were trivial.
3. Allow leaders to become buried in "background noise" by those who natter, gossip, and complain.

The first is easy to correct. As the saying goes, "Don't ask the question if you can't stand the answer." Don't give people work to do if you cannot trust them to follow through. When lay leaders start on a project, they need to have a clear assignment and to know their clergy and top lay leaders trust them to handle it. Accountability can come later.

The second has to do with showing basic respect. Some church tasks are more demanding and more important than others. But each one matters, and the persons who agree to do them need to have their efforts taken seriously. I don't think lay ministers expect applause or plaques, but they do expect to have their work noticed and honored.

The third matter, which I call "background noise," is complex. I have seen too many good-hearted lay leaders convene a meeting and immediately receive a broadside of unresolved issues, threats to leave, and passive-aggressive feints such as, "I'm not alone in feeling this way," "I've been here a long time, and I hear what people are saying."

If it were possible to diagram such exchanges, you would usually find that each person has been reading his or her script for years. Every group they join finds itself embroiled in their unresolved issues. Leaders need to be trained in how to handle such paralyzing noise.

First, while many complaints, concerns, issues, and comments are legitimate and fresh, it is possible to recognize stale noise. Leaders should compare notes on what people are saying, so that patterns of group abuse can be recognized. Tell-tale phrases like "a lot of us" usually indicate a solitary complainer trying to manipulate.

Second, a non-anxious leader can hear, take notes, and then continue on with the group's stated agenda.

Third, the leader can draw out those who aren't making noise, so that their views enter the discussion and, in all likelihood, the noise can be heard for what it is.

Finally, leaders have a duty to enforce group norms. Noise that seeks to dominate or to manipulate isn't an acceptable group behavior.

Avoid "fix-the-leader"

In worrying constantly about leadership, two unfortunate messages have been communicated. One misguided message is that clergy need to be "fixed." Better attitudes, better diets, better health, better teamwork skills, better preaching—on and on it goes, often under the guise of "clergy wellness," but with the underlying theme that if the church just had better clergy, all would be well. The other misguided message is that lay leaders need to be "fixed," too. There's less agreement on their faults—not keeping the clergy in line, not managing money well, not keeping major donors happy—but the message, again, is that the lay leadership is a mess.

I agree that leadership development is one of the "Seven Key Factors" in nurturing healthy congregations. But I think the fix-it strategy misses the point. Congregations are complex human systems. Leaders matter, but changing one leader or an entire leadership cadre won't accomplish much. The entire system needs to become healthy, not just the key leaders.

Rather than "fix" anyone, I'd suggest trying these principles:

- Healthy organizations are "flattening" the organizational chart to encourage teamwork, free-flowing relationships, and individual creativity. Even traditionally pyramidal organizations like the military and corporations find that teams perform well when allowed freedom to function responsibly outside typical command-and-control structures.

- A healthy church needs an ability to identify contextual changes promptly and to respond to them. A hierarchical or bureaucratic structure discourages such sensitivity by its tendency to assign blame, rather than learn from the unexpected. Teams and individuals "close to the ground" see more and respond better.

- A healthy church avoids centralized control, because centralized control slows communication, discourages initiative, and hampers healthy relationships. Instead, the healthy church encourages an open system, where information and ideas flow freely and rapidly and people organize themselves to deal with needs.

- Communications need to be open and transparent. No secrets or "in-crowd" knowledge.

- A healthy church expects its leaders to be innovators, not change-resisters.

CHAPTER

Communications Strategy

IT WOULD BE DIFFICULT TO OVERSTATE the importance of communications.

Our faith is grounded in "Word"—the desire of God to communicate with humanity—and the ministry of Jesus was an exercise in communications. From beginning to end, he taught, healed, served, died, and rose again in ways that brought people closer to him and to God, that enabled them to see beyond the immediate, and that were intended to form community.

As our world has grown more complex and noisy, the task of communications has become more critical. We require information in order to live effectively. We must learn to process information in order to make wise decisions. We must learn to discern and to assess information in order to maintain our freedom and integrity.

The tools of communications have grown more sophisticated, interesting, and powerful. But so has competition among users of those tools, including those who use effective communications to intimidate, to prey, and to lead us astray.

The healthy church will accept the critical importance of communications, adopt the best possible strategies and technologies for communicating effectively, and stop wasting resources on communications that don't work. We must care as much about what we say and how we say it as Jesus did.

The communications environment has changed dramatically over the past fifty years, leaving many churches stuck with costly and ineffective communications tools. The environment continues to change, as new technologies emerge and people's lives change. The most significant change, of course, is the emergence of the Internet as a primary tool for communications. That tool, in turn, changes daily.

The current Internet-centered communications environment is a "level playing field," meaning that any organization can set up an effective web site at a reasonable cost and use e-mail and messaging. Moving away from ineffective tools such as print-on-paper newsletters can save a substantial amount of money. The bad news is that a level playing field only rewards those who play effectively. The stakes are high. A congregation that refuses to embrace new technologies will find itself invisible.

Communications, in other words, epitomizes the critical nature of "best practices."

CHANGES IN THE COMMUNICATIONS ENVIRONMENT

The healthy church will accept radical changes in the communications environment and adopt strategies that reflect those changes, even if that means modifying long-standing practices. Postal is out, except for bills, junk mail, and some personal mail.

Competition at the mailbox is brutal, as personal communication moves to e-mail and the mailbox is occupied by flashy, well-designed commercial mailings that make church mailings look dowdy by comparison. In general, people expect less reward from gathering the day's mail. Some don't gather it regularly.

Postal mail isn't cost-effective for churches. They can't compete with the commercial mailers. Readership of mailed newsletters is low, except among older, longtime members. Even older members would prefer electronic mailings, according to informal studies. Reliance on a postal newsletter communicates negative messages about the church (behind the times, wordy, clergy-centered, with no room for younger people).

By contrast electronic technologies based on the Internet are:

- faster (immediate)
- cheaper (virtually no cost for e-mail)
- more reliable delivery and a relatively high rate of readership
- more attractive (color, graphics, and formatting resemble church web page).

Multipurpose communications are powerful. One e-mail with embedded links can:

- draw reader to a web site
- facilitate a transaction
- generate an e-mail response
- gather data.

Technologies

Churches should be aggressive in using the latest technologies, both to maximize return on investment and to communicate effectively. E-mail can be used for a wide range of communications needs.

E-mail newsletter

The days of the printed and mailed newsletter are over. They cost too much (over $2,000 per mailing at one large urban church, versus $15 for an e-mail version) and are read too little, especially among young and middle-aged adults. You can offer a mailed newsletter to those who prefer it, but not many will prefer it, and the e-mail version will be the centerpiece going forward.

Characteristics of the e-mail newsletter include:

- short pieces, quick read (one page)
- sent frequently (weekly, rather than monthly)
- graphically engaging
- used to drive people to web site (e.g. links to pages with content)
- leads reader to action (voice an opinion, register for event, request a contact)
- encourages downloads and other free content
- encourages "Forward this to a friend"
- offloads data management to user (e.g. change of address).

E-mail marketing

This is like the newsletter but targets specific audiences. For example, news about a men's softball team would target men of athletic age. News about a new member class would target people new to the congregation.

With a well-designed membership database, it is possible to identify market segments, such as men or women, young or elderly, new or long-time, prospects or members, and place of residence. Instead of a broadcast message, which recipients learn to ignore, use focused messages that capture recipients' attention.

Then follow these principles:

- a short e-mail about a ministry (event, class, speaker, activity) that stirs interest, draws recipient to a web site
- post content, photos, background on web site at far less cost than printing a color brochure that might or might not get read
- provide clickable response (register, indicate interest, state number in party, make payment)
- focus on gathering necessary information (such as names of those attending) via web site, thereby reducing staff data-entry requirement; this method is far more effective than the standard signup sheet placed in the lobby.

E-mail notices

In managing schedules and ministry assignments, use e-mail notices targeted to specific recipients, rather than general-audience mailings that recipients must sort through to locate their assignment.

If a response is required—to accept an assignment, for example—provide a return-mail link or drive recipient to the web site to enter information.

E-mail some personal mail

While there is still a place for the hand-written note or personal letter, e-mail has become the standard for most business communications. E-mail is more efficient to produce, less costly to send, and more prompt in delivery. Because some prefer personal letters or don't use e-mail at all, membership data should include information about members' preferences.

One word of caution: because e-mail is so easy to forward, certain uses of it should be avoided. Confidential information and pastoral information should be handled by mail or personal contact.

Effective web sites

To use the Internet effectively, the congregation needs a web site that is dynamic, promotes transactions, draws people back frequently to read new content, and avoids being a passive bulletin board or a place to present long clergy think-pieces.

Content management is critical. Users won't return to a site that rarely updates its content. Nor will they linger on pages that are dense with text. Remember: your competition isn't another church's dull web site; it is the dynamic sites that people visit for news, transactions, and services. Brevity is critical.

To update your content regularly, use a modern content management system that presents you with a page template and allows you just to enter text. This simple system will enable you to add content every day and keep your site fresh.

Follow these principles:

- Update content regularly (daily).
- Use modern content management system (e.g. open-source products like Drupal, TYPO3).
- Use short articles.
- Use graphics such as photos, and charts (optimized for fast loading).
- Avoid static content and lengthy pieces, as well as intrusive graphics.
- Present a clear message (word and graphics).

Web site design must compete effectively with other sites a member or prospect is likely to visit. That includes sites that have nothing to do with religion, but do set a standard for web presence and functionality. People don't go from one church site to another; they do their banking, check social-networking sites, and then access the church site.

To present well in this context, follow these principles:

- Update design regularly (at least quarterly) and content at least weekly, preferably more frequently.
- Learn from other web sites.
- Employ clean and simple design and fast-loading pages.
- Ensure intuitive and consistent navigation between pages.
- Assume brief page views (three to ten seconds).
- Remember that clicking matters. To keep people on your site, present links to useful information that anticipates questions the user might be asking.

Internet users expect to manage certain transactions on any web site they visit. They assume your web site is more than a bulletin board, and will want to be able to pay their pledges online, register and pay for events, and manage their personal data.

A web site offers rich opportunities for collaboration. For example:

- Engage in conversation with group, class, staff, by sending an e-mail, by entering thoughts in a blog, or by sending an instant message (if activated).
- Download files (Sunday sermons, readings, procedures, policies) and respond to them.
- Voice opinions and respond to surveys.

Collaborative services change constantly. An experienced web developer can help you add low-cost features to your web site, such as opinion-sharing.

Third-party sites, moreover, offer collaborative tools such as sharing files through Google Documents, which has recently emerged as a no-cost option for disseminating information and, if desired, enabling group editing in real time. Some youth ministers use Facebook and other social-networking sites to nurture community.

A church's web site, in other words, isn't a stand-alone venture, but is part of a dynamic web of activity in which people link to you and link away from you. Web hosting services provide a wealth of statistics on who visits your site, for how long, what pages they visit, and where they go next. These are invaluable tools enabling you to:

- track web site usage
- see what people read or do, and for how long
- drop pages and sections that have low traffic
- follow people's interests
- keep church web site in synch with other popular web sites.

A commercial e-mail handler costs more than creating groups and sending through your regular e-mail client, but the benefits of such a service justify the cost:

- get better delivery rates
- guarantee recipient has given permission
- cost is reasonable
- send automated e-mails.

Permission Marketing

Effective use of Internet-based technologies will follow principles of what is called "Permission Marketing." That is, determining in advance whether a user wants to receive your e-mail or offer and will open a pathway (through a spam filter, for example) to enable delivery.

- Offer incentives to read, receive, reply, refer.
- Pursue referrals.
- Follow deliberate path: incentives, permission, more incentives, deeper permission.
- Leverage permission to "make a sale" (e.g. attend an event).

- Avoid broadcast ("Anyone who is interested . . .") approaches; be more personal, intentional.
- Focus on renewals (e.g. renew pledge, attend event again this year).
- Continually offer opportunities to engage.

Community Building

More and more people, especially young adults, look for opportunities for "virtual community." Social-networking web sites—for example, chat rooms, discussion forums, blogging, and photo-sharing—are ways to share interests and connect with like-minded people in an efficient and safe manner, and feel some power of expression beyond a small circle of intimacy.

While faith communities tend to be profoundly incarnational, focusing on face-to-face interactions, a healthy church will offer some opportunities for community-building through communications. Web-based tools for facilitating such activities are plentiful and inexpensive, or often free.

For example, photo-sharing through a service like *flickr.com* is a way for people who experienced an event or ministry (like working on a Habitat house crew) to connect with others. A Sunday-school class, where face time is inevitably short, can keep a discussion going throughout the week through a discussion forum. Support groups can offer a log-in moderated forum, where prospective members can listen in, and eventually join in. Such opportunities should be offered through the congregation's web site, where signs of abuse can be detected, and where the existence of many community opportunities will deepen people's enthusiasm for the congregation.

The web has its own rules for civility and boundaries. Rules tend to be loose, and users can turn nasty. The church's communicators and staff will want to be attentive to signs of abuse. The pastors should drop in on all discussions from time to time, as a clear reminder of context. One way to encourage openness is to place community-building groups behind security. One must have a user ID and password to access. Permission should be granted freely, and standard information required (e-mail address, first name, last name).

All groups will need to determine whether their proceedings should be open to all or restricted to specific members. A leadership group, for example, might want to restrict access to official business, whereas a mission team might open its discussions to all.

CHAPTER

SPIRITUAL DEVELOPMENT

THE SPIRITUAL JOURNEY is personal and variable. Not everyone approaches God in the same way. Each is a pilgrim bearing different needs, wounds, experiences, ways of knowing, and ways of believing. Our approaches to God vary over time, and not necessarily in a predictable pattern by, say, age. People happen on their own to discover their "need of God." Encouragement helps, expectations hinder.

People have various understandings of what "spiritual" means, ranging from an attitude of piety to an active connection with the divine realm to specific practices such as prayer and study. Rather than argue over a "correct" definition, the healthy church affirms diverse pathways and tries to maintain an atmosphere of openness, tolerance, and mutual respect. Trying to compel conformity undermines spiritual well-being. As Paul said plainly to the Corinthians long ago, prideful claims about one's spiritual superiority are pointless.

Jesus extended invitations—"come and see"—not commands. As in the Prodigal Son parable, the road home needs to remain open. We must remember to encourage, not pressure.

Encouragement reminds the pilgrim that home awaits, points some of the ways there, and offers to help along the way.

WHY INSTRUCTION MATTERS

Instruction can help, if it remains non-directive. Spiritual development isn't a matter of acquiring expertise. It's more about developing a desire to try.

Instruction in each of the classical spiritual disciplines can show what forms trying could take, but should not rule out other ways or impose a timetable or necessary outcome.

Instruction can show an interested pilgrim how to set aside time, attention, and resources so that when the moment is right the pilgrim has some ideas about where to start.

Instruction can establish a relationship with a trusted spiritual guide.

Instruction can use stories of other people to demonstrate the experiences and feelings sometimes associated with a spiritual discipline.

YEARNING, NOT EXPERTISE

Spirituality isn't a matter of "expertise," but of yearning. Paul said God has planted in us a "spirit of adoption" that cries out to God as a child cries out to a parent.

Life, in its joys and sorrows, taps that yearning. At that point, we seek avenues for drawing closer to God. If we have developed habits, or disciplines, of spirituality, we can respond with confidence to that yearning. If we haven't developed such habits, we will need to be shown how to draw closer to God. It's like keeping a car maintained so that it's ready to drive when you need to drive. The maintenance isn't an end in itself, but an act of preparation.

COLLABORATION, NOT COMPETITION

Christians have been competing with each other over spirituality from the beginning. Paul devoted much of 1 Corinthians to that unseemly competition. It troubled him greatly.

Many church leaders have tried to identify a single spiritual path and then insist that everyone walk it. In fact, spirituality takes many pathways. Many have tried to say that some spiritual practices are superior to others, such as speaking in tongues (the Corinthians' problem) or studying Scripture a certain way. At our best, we value diversity, autonomy, and creativity. Paul identified twenty-five gifts of the Spirit, and within each of those can be found a large variety of acceptable practices. Competition over spirituality simply divides Christians and renders us ineffective in ministry. Spirituality is an occasion for collaboration.

Just as Jesus told parables from real life to make his points, so we bring God alive, to ourselves and to others, when we share our experiences of God. Even God is a story in the process of happening, not a set of definitions and demonstrable assertions. Best practices include truly listening to the other, that is, allowing them room to tell their story without fear of criticism or judgment, and telling one's story to the other in humble gratitude and discovery rather than in triumph.

SPIRITUAL DEVELOPMENT MEANS DISCIPLINES

Whether they say so or not, I think most people come to churches on a spiritual quest.

They might see their needs in more functional terms like wanting friendship, loving good music, making business contacts, or doing the right thing by their children. But the heart of their quest, I think, is a hunger for God, born of a restlessness that only God can ease.

As a savvy Presbyterian church in Texas puts on its web site: "St. Augustine wrote, 'Lord, you have made us for yourself, and our souls are restless until they find their rest in you.'"

Responding to that spiritual quest is a tricky business. We tend to get caught up in their presenting reasons. They say they want professional support, so we provide professional support groups. They say they want lively worship, so we provide lively worship. Then we are confused when they still act out their restlessness in odd behavior, neediness, and fickleness. Haven't we given them exactly what they sought?

On the other hand, we do have to meet people where they are. If someone says they're lonely, we don't serve them by going straight to pronouncing a need for a prayer group.

The best practice for responding to this delicate situation is to provide ongoing, consistent but flexible, and open-door instruction in the classical spiritual disciplines (such as prayer, meditation, fasting, and service).

By ongoing, I mean making spiritual instruction a regular part of church life, not an extravagant "special" that tries to whip up enthusiasm once a year. A class in prayer, for example, should be a fixture in church life. That way, when a person senses a need for prayer, they have a place to go for guidance.

By "consistent but flexible," I mean keeping at it, not getting discouraged when only two people come to a class on Bible study, but not getting stubborn about offering it the same way, at the same time, until people finally "get it." Clergy and other teachers should remain confident about the value of teaching Scripture, but respond to what, when, and how members are able to learn.

By "open-door," I mean making sure that spiritual instruction doesn't become precious or closed, something owned by an in-crowd. People pursue their spiritual questions in different ways and at different times. The church's responses to them must remain fresh and accessible.

Focus on Classic Spiritual Disciplines

Spirituality takes many forms. Some are widely accepted, such as prayer and worship. Some are more idiosyncratic to the individual, such as lighted candles and incense. None is to be disparaged, just because it is new or different. In seeking God, we do the best we can.

In our opinion, the healthy congregation will seek to ground its members in the classical spiritual disciplines, not to stifle other expressions, but to give them a sound starting point. It's like violinists who start by learning scales and standard literature, then go where the musical spirit leads them.

These are the classical spiritual disciples to be taught:

Prayer

Prayer means talking to God in whatever language or form one can manage (spoken words, song, writing, weeping, laughing, sighs too deep for words).

Examples from Scripture:

- The Lord's Prayer is a formal prayer with ritual language that establishes the relationship between petitioner and God.
- Miriam's Song (from Exodus 15) is an exuberant outpouring.
- Jesus' prayer in the Garden of Gethsemane is a cry from the depths.
- Psalms take several forms, such as thanksgiving, lament, and national celebration.

Reading a set prayer helps to introduce the sound of prayer, but the larger goal is to pray spontaneously from the heart. Some find that setting aside a regular time for prayer helps to underscore prayer's importance.

The point of prayer isn't to attain an orthodox understanding of God, but to stand under the umbrella of God's love.

If prayer strays from doctrine or custom, so be it. The free soul will find its way to the place where God waits.

How do you teach prayer? Life itself tends to be the first teacher. Both the joys and sorrows of life evoke in us a desire to pray. We might not call it "prayer." But listen to us when we say "Oh, God!" after a surprise, or when we look heavenward, or when we say, "Lord, help us!" in a crisis. Those are prayers, and as Paul said to the Romans, they come forth unbidden from that place in us, that "spirit of adoption," which God has planted in us. The starting point of teaching prayer, then, is to honor the instinct for prayer that we already have within us.

The second point is to ratchet down the formalism, expectations, and performance anxiety that often are associated with prayer. An honest prayer spoken from the heart conveys more depth than an eloquent prayer read from a book. A child saying, "Thank you, God, for this food," can be a livelier mealtime prayer than a grownup's well-chosen phrases. We need to let our hearts speak, in whatever language they can.

The third is to identify God as yearning to hear true words. That is, God yearns to be in relationship with us, and God wants that relationship to be grounded in full mutual acceptance: us accepting God's truth, God accepting our truth, and ourselves living in truth. In other words, no hiding. Prayer is our way out of hiding.

The fourth is to encourage an effort to try. No matter how halting, trying to pray starts us over our hurdles of shyness, self-doubt, and remorse. Praying with one other person, either a spiritual director or a trusted friend, will be a better starting point than praying in a large circle.

Finally, we need to leave room for God's many responses to prayer. Controlling nature—reversing a disease, for example—might or might not occur. The measure of prayer isn't that we get what we want, but that we were honest before God about what we needed and where we hurt and, in the process, heard the rhythms of our hearts. To experience God's responses to prayer, we need to get out of our own way, including our expectations and scripts.

Sharing glimpses of God's responses can be helpful, but must be handled with care. Spiritual triumphalism has been a longstanding problem in the Christian movement.

Study

To study effectively, we need to let go of some expectations. For many people, "study" evokes images of requirements, examinations and grades. It may suggest mastering facts or skills and thereby gaining acceptability (for a degree, job or award).

As a spiritual discipline, however, study means activities such as:

- sitting with a verse from Scripture and allowing it to speak
- exploring an idea with a group
- pursuing an insight in a written journal
- reading a useful book and allowing it to open one's eyes
- writing an essay or story that takes one deeper into a thought about God and/or life.

Study can be centered in a formal course or a self-designed pursuit. The format matters less than the discipline and determination to keep at it. Where prayer flows as it flows, study seems most helpful when it flows from intentionality.

Study can be an individual or group experience, or a combination of both. Individual study has the advantage of total freedom to explore, without any concern for affirmation or criticism. It has the disadvantage of being too self-referential and stopping short of uncomfortable discovery. Group study has the advantage of holding one accountable and stretching one's boundaries. It has the disadvantages common to any group experience, such as conflict, acting out, passive-aggressive behavior, and wasting time.

Fasting

This most ancient spiritual discipline is rarely practiced, but can be a life-changing experience.

Fasting needs to be chosen, not compelled; sought for positive reasons, not grudgingly adopted for negative reasons. It can have several meanings, but generally needs to go deeper than a child's Lenten promise to give up, say, chocolate.

As Jesus showed in the wilderness, fasting can mean going without food to the point of uncomfortable hunger (stopping well short of damage to health). This may involve giving up one meal a day for a period of time (such as the forty days of Lent), being careful not to make the two eaten meals larger in order to avoid hunger. The point of fasting is the hunger. It could also mean going without food one entire day (being careful to drink plenty of liquids), or a combination, such as one skipped meal a day and one day without any meal.

The consequences of such hunger will vary. They could include:

- a deepening of one's emotions, such as a "mellowing," a sharper temper, or sadness
- insights into oneself, one's companions, and one's world
- new compassion for those who experience hunger all the time
- a sense of "alone-ness" that gives one new appreciation for other people.

Fasting isn't for everyone. For health reasons, some people should refrain from fasting. Pregnant women, people with certain conditions and illnesses, diabetics, and others should seek a physician's advice and pay careful attention to health issues. Fasting isn't a weight-loss plan.

In the spirit of radical transparency, those who are fasting should make their family, co-workers, and significant friends aware of the fast, so that they will know how to receive the emotional changes that fasting can bring. At the same time, be careful not to make a show of fasting or to describe it pridefully.

Service

Also known as mission and servanthood, "service" means giving away one's life for the good of another person. It is the acting out of "love your neighbor."

Service includes giving away one's wealth, but it shouldn't stop there, as often happens in church mission. Service should also mean "getting your hands dirty," doing work, making sacrifices, joining hands with others to build a house or dig a trench or fight for justice. The personal dimension of service is what truly transforms both giver and receiver.

Service can change one's attitudes toward other people, not just people of different socioeconomic circumstances, but one's friends, social set, work colleagues, church friends, and family. People who serve together tend to develop deeper ties than those who party together.

Service might be the closest we come to doing what Jesus did. In his service, he healed the sick, welcomed outcasts, stood against injustice, and formed circles of caring.

Here are specific best practices for service:

Mission work matters. The healthy congregation will make a three-pronged commitment to mission:

First, it will allocate significant financial resources to mission work being done in areas of great need that might be beyond the reach of the congregation and its members. This could include, for example, tsunami relief being supported by a congregation 8,000 miles away.

Second, it will sponsor mission projects itself. These could include, for example, a homeless shelter or medical clinic using church facilities, or a tutoring ministry at a nearby school, or sending a mission crew overseas.

Third, it will send its members into the world as mission workers, so that many lives are being transformed by the doing of mission and by the receiving of care. For example, enabling parishioners to serve on house-building crews organized by others, or encouraging members to take mission initiatives at work would fall into this category.

The easiest, of course, is to allocate money. Many congregations spend too much time arguing about relatively small tokens of generosity. But even financial generosity becomes sacrificial, and life-changing, when the portion of a church budget given away to mission reaches, say, 50 percent, or individuals accept a tithe for mission as a necessary accompaniment to a tithe for local church needs.

Mission becomes harder when individuals must allocate time and effort to mission, and when they thereby find that their personal values and priorities need to be reconsidered. Mission work shouldn't be thought of as a self-improvement exercise, but the self certainly will be discomfited by serious exposure to mission needs and, in the end, made more whole. Hardest of all is for faithful people to see their entire lives as a mission field. If they can do this, they begin to make different decisions about use of their personal time and money, about lifestyle, about their duties as citizens, neighbors, and parents, and about where they stand on important political and cultural issues.

At this point, the congregation's leaders need to exercise special maturity and open-mindedness. It is tempting to say that

missional zeal leads inexorably to a specific political stance—
liberal or conservative—and to specific ways of living. The
moral life isn't that simple. Thoughtful people with generous
hearts can come down on different sides of political issues.
Church leaders need to allow room for diverse expressions.

Love, not guilt. When teaching about service and when implementing mission work, love is a more enduring motivator
than guilt.

Guilt might be easier to stimulate. A person with ample
resources can be shamed into responding to someone with
minimal resources. That guilt, however, can turn sour quickly,
leading to resentment of the needy person for being needy,
and giving grudgingly for the express purpose of quieting the
guilt. Guilt also objectifies the recipient, rather than forging a
personal bond, and places the recipient in a one-down position.
Noblesse oblige feels good, but isn't a healthy motivator.

Jesus was careful to avoid wielding the weapon of guilt. He
taught about love of neighbor, especially when the neighbor has
been cruelly treated. Giver and receiver weren't placed in a
hierarchy of power or value.

Love isn't easy to teach. Love is picked up from the
experience of seeing love in action and being loved. Hence,
it is important to offer mission work at many levels of commitment, including the least taxing, so that any individual can
step into a mission situation and be touched by it. Once love
is the motivator, they will go deeper. How could they not?
But like a child learning love by being held in a parent's arms,
we start our journey of love-motivated mission by taking
small steps.

Leadership needs to be prepared for intervention when it
sees the mission-minded resorting to guilt to recruit more
workers. Mission work is a story told, not a "should" imposed.

Giving

The spirituality of giving has been tarnished by incessant focus on church fundraising to meet organizational budgets. To reclaim the spiritual discipline of giving, we need to step away from church budgeting and experience the joy of simply being generous, in which someone else's need for support coincides with our need to give.

Eventually, one's motivation becomes gratitude, but first we need to get beyond the guilt often employed by religion. It can simply feel good to share with another person. Consider our instinct to give after a natural disaster or to a family in crisis. We feel more whole as people when we give in such a circumstance.

Giving that is motivated by guilt or shame will seek mainly to escape the negative feeling, by giving as little as possible, by blaming the recipient for being in need, or by shifting negative feelings onto someone else (scapegoating). Giving that is motivated by the positive feelings of generosity will lead not only to more generosity, but to examination of one's life and values. That self-examination, in turn, can lead to transformation of life. This is a personal journey, perhaps shared with others, but not to be compelled by peer pressure.

Giving is probably the most difficult spiritual discipline to undertake. Jesus spent two-thirds of his teaching time addressing issues of wealth and power and our need to give them away. If we believe that people killed Jesus in order to silence his voice, then these words about wealth and power are fundamentally difficult to hear.

Churches would serve their members better if they:

- refrained from adopting ambitious budgets and then asking people to pay for them as an expression of their faith. This practice, even when called a "faith budget," identifies giving, not as a response to God, but as a "should" of membership

- encouraged people to experience the joy of giving, in whatever form it takes.
- presented faith-community life as a reasonable way to act out this joy.
- lived within whatever funds were forthcoming.

Those who would lead a program of giving, such as a parish stewardship canvass, need to be givers themselves. They cannot ask for more than they themselves are willing to give. The biblical standard of the tithe—the first tenth-portion of the annual harvest—is a worthy and necessary goal. To name it, however, parish leaders need to become tithers themselves. Then their words will have sincerity and impact.

A giving program requires a certain persistence, not only because people can be hard to reach but because our human tendency is to evade people who are asking us to do something difficult. It isn't abusive to make several attempts to reach a prospect. At some point, however, persistence can cross a line and become badgering. As in other best practices, you need to learn as you go, and you need to be transparent in telling members why you are making the effort and what they can expect.

Worship

Worship is a corporate event that brings people together:

- to honor God's presence
- to join voices in song
- to pray for one another
- to hear words of encouragement, instruction, chastisement, and absolution
- to draw near to God by remembering what Jesus said and did
- to seek glimpses of the eternal in the everyday stuff of Christian fellowship.

Worship can take many forms. A healthy congregation, whatever form of worship it values, will take worship seriously and do it well.

As a spiritual discipline, worship invites the individual to enter into community. The heart of this discipline is participation:

- being part of the worship event
- helping others to worship effectively
- receiving help from others
- seeing in each other's faces glimpses of God, and hearing in each other's voices the sound of God's voice
- entering into an attitude of obedience and self-sacrifice, in not needing to get one's way, but yielding to the needs of the body.

Congregations need to stop fighting about worship. There is no one correct or holy way to worship. Fighting about worship merely drains it of vitality and trustworthiness. Worship planning shouldn't be a contest of wills, guided by ideology or seminary training or past preferences. Worship planning is entirely about what works, that is, what enables today's worshipers to approach God and to draw sustenance from the experience. Leaders need to be keen and sensitive observers of the worship environment and experience. They need to ask the question: are lives being touched and transformed?

Best practices in worship. It is difficult to talk about "best practices" in Sunday worship. People tend to feel strongly about the details and flavor of worship. Many choose a congregation precisely because the worship is what it is. They resent it when clergy or lay worship teams tinker with the Sunday service.

It's important to say, however, that "best practices" in worship don't refer to liturgical style, selection of music, worship space, or any of the other tangible specifics that we associate with worship. For the most part, those specifics aren't a factor in congregational health. You can find healthy churches that worship in every conceivable way.

More critical is whether people understand why and how they worship, and whether worship is in synch with the current personalities and needs of worshipers. For example, if people come to church after a local or national catastrophe, they expect worship that is sensitive to their feelings and makes an appropriate response to the shared experience. Whether that happens in sermon, choice of music, special elements, flowers, or lighting is up to local worship leaders. But the congregation must make some response. Similarly, if a congregation wants to serve young adults, or families with children, it cannot worship in a manner that only the elderly and tenured could appreciate. The obverse is true, as well.

Denominations have different standards for participation. A best practice is transparency, that is, clear and consistent explanations of who may participate—receive communion, receive baptism, read a lesson—and why that line has been drawn.

Another best practice is quality of execution. Whether the church is large or small, well-to-do or working-class, worship leaders can perform their duties with care and a concern for excellence. Preaching styles will vary widely, but consistent markers of excellence are clear thinking, effective delivery (as a congregation understands effectiveness), and attention to impact.

Confession

Confession is an approach to God made in humility, openness, and submission. It is laying one's sins before God with the assurance that God will show mercy.

Public confession is practiced regularly in both liturgical and non-liturgical churches. The sacrament of Confession (usually private) is less widely practiced, except in Roman Catholicism. (In the Episcopal Church it is called Reconciliation of a Penitent.)

ROLES OF THE CONFESSOR (THE ONE HEARING A CONFESSION) ARE:

- to restore oneself to right relationship with God and with other people, especially one's faith community
- to remove the burden of guilt, so that one can live freely
- to make amends to God and, emboldened by that, to make amends to those hurt by one's sin.

PURPOSES OF CONFESSION ARE:

- to listen with a non-judgmental attitude
- to provide a safe place where people can face their frailties
- to provide the assurance of forgiveness
- to call the penitent to new life and wholeness.

Personal confession, made in one's prayer time, has merit, too. The key is honesty with oneself.

The pastor needs to set aside regular times to hear confessions. This will be new behavior in many churches and will need to be taught, with the leadership explaining the practice, explaining its costs and benefits, explaining God's desire that confession occur, and explaining the pastor's role and boundaries.

Silence

Silence means more than the absence of noise or of sound altogether. Silence doesn't require one to leave a noisy street-corner and make a short-term pilgrimage to an isolated retreat center. Silence is a discipline.

We need to be taught the benefits of silence.

- Create a quiet space for hearing one's own soul speak.
- Create an empty space for God to fill.
- Let God do and be whatever God wants.

We need to be taught the character of silence.

- It is a necessary contrast to a noisy world.
- It is a deliberate act to get outside oneself in order to comprehend oneself—in listening for another's sound, one hears one's own heart more clearly.

In addition to teaching individuals how to be silent, congregations should offer occasions of corporate silence, such as walking a labyrinth, a silent retreat, or Lenten silent periods. Those who have learned the practice of silence should be offered opportunities to speak about it.

Seeking a Balanced Spiritual Life

Congregations should offer regular instruction on each spiritual discipline, to show possible ways and examples from life. In addition, congregations should offer opportunities to act, such as mission work and prayer vigils. Doing and learning need to go hand in hand. Otherwise, the doing loses its foundation, or the learning becomes sterile and precious.

The point isn't to promote a single way, but several ways that work together to promote spiritual well-being. For example:

- confession opens one's eyes and heart to distance from God
- prayer seeks to bridge that distance
- mission follows as a way to express gratitude for feeling closer to God
- stewardship follows as a way to act out Christian values in one's personal life
- fasting follows as a way to rethink one's life in basic ways.

Clergy should offer spiritual direction focused on:

- getting beyond obstacles
- developing a personal plan for spiritual discipline
- establishing a healthy relationship between pastor and congregant (better than the usual power-based relationship).

It is especially important that clergy offer spiritual direction to all key leaders. It will establish a proper relationship between clergy and leadership, and it will build trust. Spiritual direction will shift the focus of leadership from organizational management to mission and servanthood. The congregation should steadily expand a core leadership cadre who understand spiritual vitality as essential.

Spiritual vitality means going deeper in one's faith and making one's faith an offering to the world. It isn't a personal triumph or accomplishment. Those who brag about their spiritual depth are making an idol of certain forms and behaviors that they happen to like.

CHAPTER

YOUNG ADULTS MINISTRIES

A HEALTHY FAITH COMMUNITY will serve all age groups, of course. Right now, however, young adults (aged 22–30) tend to be absent from mainline churches and are little understood as a potential constituency. In order to have a vibrant future, many congregations need to focus special energy on young adults. Once balance is attained, perhaps this constituency won't require such targeting.

Here's why:

- A balanced age mix is critical to the future stability of a congregation. The rising average age of mainline congregations—currently estimated at 62 years old—simply isn't a sustainable trend.

- A lively presence of young adults will keep the congregation current with the needs and trends that will shape future ministry.

- Through targeting young adults, congregations will embrace key principles like responsiveness to a changing market, seeing needs through others' eyes, the need for broad diversity of offerings, and nimbleness in changing design. This will keep the congregation open to new ideas. Or, said another way, it will prevent the congregation from simply growing older (rising average age) and losing touch with emerging constituencies.

- Young adults are difficult to reach through normal avenues.

Why are young adults absent from so many congregations? Young adults don't seem to be averse to Christian faith, but they aren't seeing traditional church membership as the primary path for expressing or seeking faith.

They are more likely to:

- sign on with a mission opportunity, whether church-related or not
- engage in faith-centered interactions on the Internet
- attend occasional events at non-demanding large churches with little or no denominational overhead
- see faith as something to be addressed later, perhaps when they marry and have children
- see church as an irritating venue where smug people argue
- see mainline churches as tightly controlled by older generations
- turn away from the growing conservatism of many churches, especially in moral issues such as sexuality and immigration.

On the other hand, in a diversity that confuses many older adults, some young adults are flocking to conservative congregations precisely because they seem sure of themselves and offer firm answers in a fluid world. Single-track programs don't address this diversity.

Ministry to young adults requires intentionality and priority. It won't be easy. A serious effort to speak to, listen to, and learn from young adults will take a congregation to places it hasn't gone before, such as heavily web-centered communications and community-building. The congregation will need to let go of control, and allow ministries to develop that don't resemble local tradition.

Young adults are likely to be more serious about their faith than less. A congregation that has enjoyed good times and easy ministries will need to rethink its approach if it wants to communicate seriousness to young adults. It isn't anything as easy as adding a "hip" service to the Sunday mix.

As with any group, it is critical that we try to understand young adults. Without drifting too deeply into stereotypes, here are some factors worth considering:

- As they go from college to first jobs, and from domicile to domicile, young adults can "fall off the radar," as it were. Mailing addresses, employers, and other usual identifiers get out of date.

- Because they tend to be work-centered and not yet affiliated with institutions like schools and youth sports, young adults miss the hooks that churches often use.

- Because their schedules are less consistent, young adults might not fit into existing church schedules.

- Because they tend to float among several friendship groups—work, sports, former college friends—they might not be as reachable through "customer evangelism" as they will be later in life.

- With marriage typically happening later, perhaps after 30, if at all, the ways into community life known by earlier generations might not be available.

- The life changes of the 20s are substantial and often lead to painful consequences, such as loneliness, over-commitment to work, separation from former friends or even from spouses, and financial stress.

- It can be a time of heightened personal need but reduced openness to expressing need or acting on it. New adults don't want to be put into the "child" position again.

- Former support networks might have been left behind and new networks not yet developed, except possibly online.

- Young adulthood is often not a time when faith and church are perceived as needs.

- Many young adults believe, rightly or wrongly, that they have just this one decade to prove themselves professionally. Other expressions, including church, are put on hold.

- With health still strong and career options open, stresses can feel manageable and not require any "outside assistance," such as a faith community or a God.

- If they grew up in churchgoing families, that familiar activity might seem linked to childhood, not to life itself, and tied to a specific congregation, not something one can seek in a new locale.

Older members tend to resist adapting congregational life to young adults. It would shift the focus from themselves, which is counterintuitive in today's culture, especially among the "baby boomers" now entering late middle-age and reluctant to give up the center stage they have known all of their lives.

Some attitudes that may be common among older adults:

- The young should wait their turn.

- The older know better.

- Those who pay the bills deserve preferential treatment.

- The needs that young adults experience seem trivial to many older adults, who didn't have a 20s experience like this or have forgotten theirs.

- Young adults can be intimidating with their health, physical attractiveness, and career zeal.

WHO ARE THEY?

In order to minister effectively to young adults, we need to be clear about who they are. ("Anyone younger than I am" isn't an adequate identifier.) We are defining young adults in these terms:

- ages 22–30
- post-college
- probably not yet parents
- probably not yet homeowners
- starting out in careers.

This decade shows certain characteristics:

- a decade of stress and maturation
- adjusting to life on their own, often in a new environment, without support structures of family and school
- facing adult accountability for the first time
- dealing with stressors like loneliness, not belonging, feeling disconnected
- dealing with grown-up relationship issues
- handling sexual pressures
- some ready for marriage, some not; friendship circles changing dramatically
- sometimes over-committed to career
- completing move away from parents' values and politics, and now adopting their own
- targeted for enormous commercial energy and manipulation
- just starting to address questions of who they are and what they want out of life.

These characteristics aren't uniform, of course. Part of being a young adult is to defy easy categorization. Nor do these characteristics apply evenly throughout the age range. Even though the average age of starting marriage is nearing 30, many marry earlier in this decade. Many start families. A healthy congregation will look closely at its actual and potential young adult constituents to see them as they are.

We need to address some misconceptions:

- Age range: A range of 20–40 is too broad. Young adults are defined by being in early stages of certain life transitions (career, residence, marriage).

- Worship: "Trendy worship" might miss the mark. Many young adults are looking for tradition, but offered in a lively and engaging format. Some want contemporary worship, because they perceive its message as being more pertinent.

- Self-centeredness: Young adults are often seen as self-centered and are treated that way by commerce. In fact, idealism is strong at that age.

- Interests: This age group is often seen as interested only in careers and fun. However, other concerns are evident, too, such as the search for meaning in life and in religion, new circles of friendship, a sense of belonging.

- Sunday is sufficient: Increasingly, the needs that people bring to a faith community must be addressed in ways other than Sunday morning worship. This is true for all age groups, but especially for young adults. The older generations who tend to lead congregations will need to rethink their focus—often exclusive focus—on Sunday morning.

FOCUS ON FIVE AREAS

Reaching, welcoming, and serving young adults isn't necessarily a continuation of current approaches. Being friendly and sincere won't be enough. Five specific areas need addressing:

1. Online tools to engage and to build community

   - e-mail lists and permission marketing
   - web site

2. Small-group formations

   - strong social component (Sunday brunch, dancing, theater outings)
   - frequent, consistent, and not too large
   - low pressure; focus on invitation and regularity

3. Age-related activities (e.g. athletics)

   - self-led
   - reflect scheduling realities of age group
   - test and measure (no formula works in every setting)

4. Age-appropriate worship

   - needs to be studied carefully
   - not as simple as "guitar songs"
   - study what other churches are offering
   - test and measure
   - be sincere and true to overall tradition
   - consider possibility that regular service needs to be updated, rather than a separate "young adult service" be offered
   - understand that worship's importance varies widely within this age group

- in brief: don't place high expectations on worship as the core of ministry to this age group

5. Mission activities
   - respond to idealism in this age group
   - way to meet like-minded people
   - new forms of socialization
   - prove flexibility and openness of congregation

STAFF ROLES

Congregations always compete for the attention of staff, especially clergy. Staff needs to make sure that young adults get their share. All clergy need to greet young adults by name, to promote visibility and belonging.

Clergy need to communicate that this group is a priority because they matter, not because older adults want them to "save the parish."

Include young adults in leadership, but be patient with travel schedules or wandering focus. Be flexible, and be prepared for new ways of communicating, forming community, and seeking values.

Engage Young Adults in Identifying Obstacles

It is important to engage young adults in identifying obstacles, if any, to full and enthusiastic participation in regular congregational worship and activities. Older adults shouldn't assume they know what young adults think, want, or need. It is better to let the young adults speak for themselves.

Rather than surveying many young adults and running the risk of communicating uncertainty, use a focus group of a few trusted young adults to glean useful insights. As they call on young adults, clergy should listen for needs and yearnings, especially those that might require new responses. Then, using the "test and measure" principle, try some fresh approaches and see what the response is.

For any of this to succeed, the overall congregation must be ready to hear what the focus group says and to modify current offerings in response. If young adults seem uninterested or drift away, ask them why.

SEEK TO KNOW YOUNG ADULTS

As we learn time and again, understanding any person or group is difficult. Not only are we tempted to project our own selves onto them, but they insist on revealing themselves selectively, sometimes not at all.

Perhaps the least understood group in any congregation is young adults. Not because they are an unusually complex cohort—everyone is complex—but because church leaders, indeed most current church members, are so much older. With the average age of parishioners in mainline Protestant denominations edging past 60, most members are one to two generations removed from those aged 22–30.

While they might remember their 20s—falling in love, partnering for life, starting a first job, buying first car and first house, changing careers, tasting first failure—they don't fully comprehend what it means to be 25 today.

They might see the angst—loneliness, career worries, sexuality issues—but not the zest, the excitement of today's young adult world. They might see young adults leaving small towns and suburbia and worry about the future of those venues, but not see young adults pouring into large cities and downtown lofts, not owning cars or watching television, having large families, but not planning to return to the suburbs when children come along.

Church leaders wait hopefully for young adults to discover their need for church. What they might not see is that young adults have discovered a need for faith, values, and meaning. They just aren't pursuing it by attending Sunday worship at a local church.

If they do attend church, it's likely to be one of the so-called "emerging churches" or a non-denominational church, which has worked hard to prepare itself for young adults. If our churches are to have a future and not just age gracefully past the possibility of new life, two things need to happen.

First, church leaders need to make a systematic, sustained, and humble effort to understand young adults. I mean work at it, and work smart. Don't just talk to a few and think you know enough. Talk to many—better yet, listen to them—read the literature, examine what churches with young constituencies are doing, get out of your own way.

Second, be prepared to adapt. The church might be the last institution in our culture that thinks staying the same is a good strategy. If you want to have a future, you need to position yourself for the future that is happening.

Like it or not, older adults need to stop controlling church practices to suit their tastes. In the end, being welcoming to younger people will benefit the entire congregation, including older parishioners. After all, those who care about the church will want it to stay healthy and vital, during their lifetimes and beyond.

CHAPTER

THE LISTENING CHURCH

CHURCHES HAVE A MESSAGE that they feel obligated to proclaim, as well as ways of being that they feel obligated to continue. An additional reality needs to be taken into consideration: the questions that people themselves are asking.

If given an opportunity to raise their hands, as it were, church members tend to have questions that they would ask of God and about God. Sometimes those questions are quite different from the questions that the congregation is answering. A healthy congregation wants to listen to those questions, as well as to questions coming into the faith community from the world outside.

In an extensive survey of churchgoers in many regions and denominations, we discovered that their questions tended to reflect yearning and curiosity, rather than anger or frustration. Their content tended to be basic and rarely referenced standard church concerns—or arguments—like doctrine and cultural/political issues. Typical questions include:

- Who is God?
- Where does God live?

- What is God's purpose for my life?
- Why do people suffer, especially children?
- Will my life work out (will I get married, get a job, have good health)?

Rarely do questions deal with church controversies—unless the person is steered that way by the church. Nor do questions deal with doctrine or institution. On their own, people ask more basic questions of God.

A healthy church listens to the questions people are asking. Leaders don't force an agenda onto people. Leaders start by hearing where people's yearnings and curiosities lie.

An effective approach is simply to ask: "What one question would you ask of God?"

Method 1: Pass out 3 x 5 card at Sunday worship and other gatherings. Don't explain up front, to avoid steering the questions.

Method 2: If you have an e-mail newsletter, use it to ask the question, and provide a link so that people can reply easily.

Questions are catalogued by content and feel, so that patterns can be discerned. For example:

- Content:
  - Purpose
  - Faith
  - Sexuality
  - Peace
  - Leadership
  - Church
  - Death
  - Suffering
  - Doctrine

- Feel:
  - Yearning
  - Curiosity
  - Anger
  - Frustration
  - Fear

A healthy church adapts itself to answering those questions. Doing so isn't the church's only agenda, but a promising starting point, especially in discerning direction for ministries and programs. Clergy can preach to the questions, especially when they see patterns, such as numerous questions about war or children's suffering. Educators can structure education offerings, both for children and for adults, around the questions.

If this is done transparently (people know the questions and why they are being answered), people will form an impression of the congregation as a "listening church." People will hear other people's questions and learn to respect diversity within the congregation, and preaching and teaching will take on new urgency.

ORGANIZATIONAL STRUCTURE TO SUPPORT LISTENING

Congregations need to be intentional about adopting organizational structures that affirm the asking of questions, facilitate the act of listening, and communicate that listening isn't just crisis management, but a fundamental commitment to be responsive.

That means, to the extent possible within the denomination, a non-hierarchical leadership structure. Leadership focused on power and control isn't conducive to listening, and members sense when they are viewed as "foot soldiers" of someone else's agenda. They prefer to be co-workers in ministries that reflect their questions.

Instead of a standard pyramidal structure where power flows up to top leaders and directions flow down, a healthy church operates "horizontally," with a network of self-organizing groups and individuals who pursue a broad array of ministries on the basis of shared interest and autonomy. Leaders serve by providing a supportive environment where people feel free to take initiative and to function independently but within congregational norms.

The focus should be on small covenant communities where people can form significant, faith-centered relationships. (See Chapter 1, Membership Development, particularly the section on Small Groups.)

- People do a better job of listening than institutions do, because institutions tend to be deaf except to signals like money and complaint.

- Personal needs, yearnings, and desires to serve are more likely to be expressed freely in a setting with some intimacy and trust.

- Small groups might not have the heft to undertake solutions or initiatives, but they do provide a free-thinking environment where ideas can be floated, tested, refined, and then passed along for others to consider as well.

- Authentic listening is a "call and response" process, in which questions are encouraged and honored, and then made part of the group's life. A hierarchical institution can rarely do more than harvest one-way communications.

WORSHIP TO SUPPORT LISTENING

Worship traditions and expectations vary widely among denominations. Some faith traditions are freer than others to design worship so that it responds directly to people's questions.

To the extent possible, all worship should reflect the questions that people are asking. For example:

- After a national or local tragedy, it would be artificial to present worship that ignored the trauma that people are feeling.
- After a spate of deaths, or some high-profile bouts of illness, a healthy church will want to respond publicly, not just go about "business as usual."
- A congregation with many young families will want to address issues common to young families, such as life-purpose, concern about public schools, time and money management.

Preachers should speak to the questions that people are asking. Any good sermon stitches together three elements: Scripture, people's lives, and events in the larger world. A "Listening Church" sermon would start with the questions people are asking—such as "who is God" or "why do people suffer"—and then seek responses in Scripture and in experience.

This happens naturally during a community crisis. At other times, it can help to identify the question being addressed, to show that this is a pressing matter to some congregants and therefore of concern to all.

Instead of having every Sunday service be alike, planners can vary content and tone to reflect different sorts of questions, ranging from somber to uplifting, from yearning to angry. Establish a worship environment that promotes exploration and imagination, not rigidity and requirement, and ground worship design in the questions people are asking. Some questions lend themselves to liturgical expression. For example:

- If people are asking about suffering, the service can include ministry of healing, songs about suffering, message of God's steadfastness and our hope.

- If people are asking about life purpose, the service can include baptismal or membership covenant, witnesses to faith at work in daily work and life, music about mission.

Some questions go beyond words—such as questions about hope or loneliness—and could benefit from expression in dance, art, or chamber music. Questions that reflect interests of children—often shared by adults—could form the basis for a children-led liturgy.

ACTING ON QUESTIONS

A commitment to acting on members' questions leads in many directions, from program planning to pastoral care to facilities. In general, the issue that needs to be addressed is: does this program (ministry, staffing, or facilities decision) respond to questions that people actually are asking? For example, if people are dealing with financial insecurity, does refurbishing the church parlor respond to their questions? If people are dealing with anxiety about time management, is a decision to resurrect the Fall Bazaar a responsive idea?

To promote awareness of other people and consensus in ministries, share the questions people are asking. Within normal bounds of confidentiality, enable the entire membership to know the questions being asked in their midst.

It helps everyone to know the pain and joys that others are experiencing. That's one reason people tend to respond so well to stories about death and family tragedies. They know the question and can imagine a response. It helps people to accept diversity and change when they know the human drama behind those phenomena. It isn't just the pastor meddling, it is movement of the human spirit.

Discuss trends. One way for people to understand their world is to see its impact on individual lives. For example:

- A pattern of layoffs can seem cold and uninteresting, until you know that people near you in the pew are asking questions about their jobs and economic security.
- If older members knew the loneliness-related questions being asked by many young adults, they might be more receptive to welcoming them and to rethinking congregational life to meet their needs.

LOVING STARTS IN LISTENING

In eighteen years of parish ministry and twelve years of church consulting, I have yet to meet a pastor or lay leader who didn't want to be effective. They want to do the job right. They want to have healthy churches. So often, however, they haven't been shown where to start and how to proceed.

One sign of this is a basic, and thoroughly flawed, paradigm that seems active in many churches: clergy feel called to provide what they want to provide. If they feel called to promote a certain activity or educational pursuit or liturgical focus or pastoral emphasis, they have a right to do so.

"Express yourself," some say. "Go where your heart is. Do what you know how to do." With the spread of lay ministries, many laity are feeling called to do the same.

The result, more often than not, is a disconnect between what service providers want to do and what their constituents want to receive. Members feel stifled, unheard, ignored, patronized, and unloved. Imagine being thirsty for water, and someone offers you salty crackers because that is what they feel called to offer.

The best practice is to listen first. The wise leader starts by listening to fellow leaders and then, with them, listening to the led. A smart leader could guess what people would say, but a wise and compassionate leader gives them the opportunity to say it. Feeling heard and respected is an essential condition for agreeing to work with someone and/or to follow them.

Yes, listening can be time-consuming. But not listening and then having to deal with missed signals, unresponsive constituents, failed programs, and conflict will be even more time-consuming and costly.

Listening doesn't mean being slavish to fickle opinion; leaders do need to lead. It means knowing what your people are worried about—job security, public schools, retirement savings, loneliness—and then offering services that respond to those worries.

It means honoring different languages, different ways of receiving spiritual guidance, different pathways to faith shaped by life experience.

Effective pastors know this to be true in pastoral care. The best expression of love and mercy starts in being present and listening. The same is true in all aspects of ministry. Ordination or election to a church council doesn't confer a license to do whatever one pleases. It confers permission to listen and then to respond.

CHURCHES SERVE COMMUNITIES

No church is an island. The healthy church serves its community—village, town, city, state, nation. Here are some signs of effective servanthood:

- The church suffers as the community suffers. After 9/11, it would have been inconceivable for any New York City church to go about "business as usual." The same should be true when a factory closes, violence hits a school, racial tension erupts, immigrants are rounded up, and soldiers die in battle. A suffering community needs to see its suffering reflected in and lifted up by its churches.

- The church grows as its surrounding community grows. Each denomination has a particular mission in American life. Each congregation has a unique and necessary voice in its community. Our strength is our balance and diversity. If a community is gaining in population, then its churches should be growing in membership, too.

- The church does what the community needs doing. If children need recreation, churches should build gyms and ball fields. If people need food, churches should provide food. If two-income families need child care, churches should open nursery schools. If the community needs meeting places, churches should roll out the carpet—even if the carpet then gets worn out.

- The servant church should say what needs to be said. That won't mean a single voice. Denominations disagree about almost everything, and within congregations, members disagree. But disagreement shouldn't mean a call to silence. Churches should enter the community's debates, if only to make sure that all viewpoints are heard.

- Churches serve segments but love all. It is inevitable that each church will serve a segment of the community. That loyalty to its few, however, shouldn't be expressed as triumphalism over the many, or smugness about being a "righteous remnant," or disdain for those who worship elsewhere or don't worship at all. We need to get beyond our history of factional hubris.

CHAPTER

METRICS

THE BASIC PRINCIPLE OF WEB COMMERCE is "test and measure." Do the best you can in discerning a need and designing a product or service to meet it, then try your idea and see if it works. This principle is directly applicable to church wellness.

Rather than argue about proposed solutions—which tends to be a contest of wills between solution proponents, rather than an objective assessment of ideas—let the marketplace speak.

Behind the basic principle of "test and measure" is a conviction that an institution ought to do what works and stop doing what doesn't work. As a steward of limited resources, a church cannot justify continuing programs that few are attending or offering services that few utilize.

We need objective tools for discerning what works, what doesn't work, and what needs to change. Those aren't tools for pouncing and blaming, but for assessing our performance in meeting actual needs. We call those tools "metrics," or measurements.

Measurements ease our fear of failure by promising prompt discernment of false assumptions, inadequate planning, or conceptual gaps, and they facilitate prompt remediation. An idea's proponent won't be "hung out to dry" with an idea that has missed the mark but cannot be dropped. "Test and measure" recognizes that reality isn't always responsive to our plans and actions. Nor are our planning and execution flawless.

A second basic principle is that, for metrics to be indicative and trustworthy, we must gather data regularly and fearlessly. Numbers need to be accurate and consistently gathered. A negative number isn't to be avoided for fear of offending someone or admitting failure. Measuring needs to be a staff priority to ensure consistent and accurate data collection.

After verifying the accuracy of data, leaders need to make the data available to all. The data and resulting accountability must be shared by the entire congregation. We need to remove data as a political weapon. When people disagree, as they always will, let it be about opinions, not facts—or about analysis of facts, not the numbers themselves.

ACCURATE NUMBERS COUNT

Accurate measurements are critical to a congregation's well-being.

Numbers represent people. A change in membership count means the congregation is serving more or fewer people. A change in Sunday attendance means greater or lesser impact on people's lives. A change in non-Sunday participation means something is changing at home, or at work, or in how church matters to people. In trying to understand such numbers, you are taking a big step in understanding your people and in understanding your congregation's effectiveness.

While every manager in every organization is tempted to fudge the numbers, you gain far more by measuring accurately and consistently. Numbers signal critical transitions. A change in young children's participation, for example, will signal not only next year's Sunday School staffing needs, but long-term space requirements, potentially disruptive shifts in average adult age, and new faces in leadership.

Numbers are a key indicator of outcomes. For example, your congregation added a third service to relieve over-crowding. To know if it worked, you need to measure how many you anticipated at the new service and how many partici-pated. Should you be adding space instead?

In dealing with limited resources, congregations need to allocate money and staff time to ministries and activities that work. Positive or negative trends in measureable outcomes must guide that assessment. Otherwise, you find yourself in personality conflicts. The measure of a ministry isn't whether a few opinion-setters liked it, but did people respond to it and did their response justify the cost and effort?

Long-term trends in key metrics like attendance and mem-bership offer important insights into the overall effectiveness of staff, lay leadership, programs, facilities, and other variables. Decisions about future spending need to take those outcomes into account.

For numbers to work for you, two things need to happen:

First, parish leaders need to avoid any hint of defensiveness about the numbers. A decline in Sunday attendance could have a dozen explanations. But no causes will be sought, or reme-died, unless leaders agree to value the numbers.

Second, the numbers need to be painstakingly accurate. "I guess we had 500 in church today" is meaningless. Was it 520 or 475? Numbers must be not only accurate, but consistent, meas-ured in the same way every time.

Over time, numbers tell the congregation's story. I remem-ber a congregation in which the leaders were convinced their parish was on a plateau. In fact, by every metric I could exam-ine, they were in a seven-year decline. Big difference.

I remember another that thought paying its bills was the best measure of health. In fact, financial giving is a lagging indicator. Attendance changes first, then membership, and then giving. By the time a decline hits giving, the original causes of systemic decline are difficult to discern and it seems time only for blaming and cost-cutting.

Because numbers are so important, churches should train their counters. They need instruction in how to count crowds, methods for ensuring accuracy, and appropriate tools for entering data and transmitting it to relevant staff.

DEVELOPING USEFUL MEASUREMENTS

Since religion provokes strong feelings and church participation tends to be emotion-laden and often volatile, we need metrics that are durable and reliable enough for us to hear above the "noise" of our feelings.

That means, first, that we need numerical measures that can be tracked and charted. For example, attending a class is a better measure than saying one likes or doesn't like the class. Track behavior, then ask why. People's willingness to teach Sunday school is a better measure than a goal statement saying Sunday school is important.

Second, we need measures where a variance has identifiable meaning. For example, if volunteer count on, say, a yard cleanup day declines steadily for several years, it might mean this ministry needs to be stopped or changed. If giving to a capital project lags far behind giving to operations, it might indicate the capital project lacks adequate support. Changes over time tend to reveal more than simple slice-of-time measurements.

Third, meaningful measures are those that involve people's behaviors or choices. Opinion surveys mean less than behavior tracking. People vote with their feet, as they say, not with their mouths. In a religious system where nice, passive, and polite are operative values, people often say one thing and do another; the former to avoid criticism or feeling out of step, the latter as an expression of their actual values.

Fourth, we need measures that are useful for macro-level trends and micro-level behaviors. Sunday attendance, for example, is a useful *macro* measurement, because it shows high-level trends and allows for adequate budgeting, staffing, and planning. When tracked by age group, gender, and frequency of attendance, Sunday attendance is a useful *micro* measurement, because it shows segmented behavior and allows fine-tuning of staffing and planning.

Finally, it is important to gather the same metrics every week, every month, every year, as appropriate. One-time measures don't mean as much as consistent measurements over time. One-time measures can reveal a gap between expectation and actuality. But measurements over time show trends in actual response. It is trends that matter, not isolated numbers.

SOME USEFUL METRICS

Here are some useful metrics, organized by category. The purpose and use of each are presented in brief summary to stimulate your thinking.

Once you have started implementing metrics, you will identify other measures worth taking. Remember that any useful metric must be taken accurately and consistently, and that trends over time tend to be more revealing than a single count.

Attendance Metrics

TOTAL SUNDAY ATTENDANCE

Method: Count all adults and children in church on a Sunday, including children not in worship but on the premises in nursery or class.

Purpose & Use: This is a basic measure of activity. It tends to be a more valuable indicator than membership. Trends over time matter more than a single Sunday's count. When correlated with demographic data in a service area, metric indicates performance in comparison with prevailing growth or decline. A 10 percent growth in Sunday attendance looks positive if the surrounding population has grown, say, 5 percent over the same period, but negative if area growth was 20 percent.

KEY SUNDAYS ATTENDANCE

Method: Count all adults and children in church on key Sundays: Christmas, Easter, Pentecost, opening of Fall program.

Purpose & Use: Key Sunday vs. normal Sunday indicates rate of participation. (400 on Easter and 150 on regular Sunday suggests a 38 percent participation rate, a number that can be tracked over time to indicate market penetration.)

MIDWEEK EVENT ATTENDANCE

Method: Count all adults and children attending supper, class, and/or worship on a standard midweek day.

Purpose & Use: Growing congregations emphasize midweek gatherings as community-building and educational time. This metric measures success in reaching people. When correlated with Total Sunday Attendance, metric indicates success in drawing people to midweek event.

SPECIAL EVENT ATTENDANCE

Method: Count all adults and children who attend special annual events, such as parish picnic, beach retreat, founders' day, saint's day, yard-work day, Thanksgiving supper.

Purpose & Use: When measured consistently over time, trends will indicate rising or falling appeal. When correlated with cost of event and staffing required, metric will suggest cost-effectiveness of event.

Tracking Results

Useful metrics will tend to track these kinds of behaviors:

Participation, such as:

- What is attendance like at regular events (e.g. worship, Sunday school, Wednesday supper, ongoing groups' meetings)?
- What is attendance like at annual events (e.g. retreats, beach weekend)?
- What is attendance like at ad hoc events (e.g. a dance, a fundraising dinner)?
- Do members seem more or less engaged in congregational life?
- Has any faith-related participation shifted to opportunities outside the congregation? Why?
- Do some members (age group, gender group, socioeconomic group) seem more or less engaged than others?

Ministries, such as:

- Sunday school teachers and how many calls it took to recruit annual staff
- volunteers for ongoing mission work (e.g. Habitat house)
- volunteers for ad hoc mission work (e.g. assist flood victims)

- acolytes and how many calls it took to recruit them
- distribution of participation (new members, longtime members, women, men, age cohorts).

Giving, such as:

- pledge data (total amount pledged, number of giving units, average pledge, numbers of new, increased, decreased, and terminated pledges)
- special appeals
- ongoing mission appeals
- capital projects.

OUTCOME-BASED DECISION-MAKING

The goal of metrics is outcome-based decision making.

We must either change or discontinue things that aren't working. That means learning from our failure, not hiding from it. There is no shame in failure. Failure is a better teacher than success. As faithful stewards, we must allocate resources according to what works, not according to habit, conflict-avoidance, or emotional bullying. We must seek to analyze outcomes, not explain them away or perpetuate ministries for fear of offending ministry providers.

Metrics will gain acceptance over time through experience of the benefits they provide. As we grow accustomed to objective forms of accountability, we will encounter less defensiveness, less apology, and more desire to know reality and to respond to it. When leaders behave less defensively, they will experience more trust in their actions, because members will know the basis on which decisions were made. And remember, metrics themselves need to be measured. Some will prove less valuable than others and need to be dropped.

OUTCOMES, NOT INTENTIONS

Church planning starts with intentions: dreaming, imagining, conceptualizing, applying values, making plans, assigning roles, anticipating success. Then come results, or outcomes. The plan succeeds or fails, or waffles frustratingly between outright success and outright failure.

The tendency, in churches and in other venues, is to restate intentions, to reaffirm a determination to accomplish a desired goal using preferred methods, to dig in stubbornly for another try—in other words, to ignore outcomes. We didn't mean for this negative outcome to happen; therefore, we just need to try harder. Grit and determination might well be called for. But unless we examine outcomes, we will never know. We might just repeat the same scenario, experience the same negative results, and lose confidence.

Two obstacles get in our way:

One is our inherent difficulty in admitting failure. We feel diminished by failure, rather than energized. We know from experience that failure brings forth blaming and punishment. We will explain away our failures, rather than learn from them.

The second obstacle is "turf." Any plan or method develops a constituency. The "owners" of that plan will be reluctant to let it go, even when it fails again and again.

A "best practices" commitment to accurate and consistent metrics and to learning from outcomes can surmount both obstacles. Metrics don't lie. If one person came to an event, one person came. It doesn't matter whether the dream was ten or fifty. The reality was one. It's hard to hide from accurate measurements.

If metrics are seen as a community matter—valued and assessed by all, in a true sharing of accountability—then no ministry planner needs to avoid blame or punishment by clinging to a failed idea. It becomes easier to say, "All right, we tried this, it didn't work, so let's try another way."

LEARNING FROM FAILURE

As we've observed before, failure is a better teacher than success. It is also more demanding.

For example, a church tries to recruit new members with a monthly Newcomers Brunch. For a time, the meal seems to succeed—at least, enough people attend to justify the effort. But then, one month, only one person accepts the invitation. The brunch needs to be cancelled, which disappoints the one who accepted and frustrates the several who were planning to host. What now? Hope this was a one-time blip? Question the process? Blame seasonal factors?

In my opinion, this failure should cause the entire enterprise to be examined. Not to assign blame, but to understand. Why did this brunch not succeed? And did the ones that people attended actually constitute a success?

The invitation method was low-energy: an announcement on Sunday, a sign-up sheet in the lobby, and one personal letter. Is a low-energy approach adequate? Should the hosts have been telephoning and making follow-up calls? People appreciate being wooed, after all.

Leaders also need to examine the brunch concept. Let's say the congregation had twenty visitors a month. Of those, ten gave an address (postal or e-mail) and five attended the brunch. All five eventually joined the parish. Five out of five seems a good result, right? No, the actual yield is five out of twenty, or 25 percent, not a good yield. If the visitors had been called on right away, the yield would have been closer to 90 percent. Getting addresses on only 50 percent of the visitors automatically cuts in half the potential benefit of recruitment efforts.

The failure of this one event opens the door to several shifts in tactics. For example:

- doing better at gathering addresses of visitors
- trying more direct methods of issuing invitations
- making invitees feel special by avoiding the dreaded "anyone who wants . . ." of a public announcement
- noticing who talks with the visitor on Sunday and inviting that person to the brunch, too.

Without the outright failure, none of these next steps would have occurred. The former program, even though not a success, would have remained below the pain threshold and been ignored.

Conclusion

IF YOU HAVE HEARD NOTHING ELSE in this book, I hope you have heard these three critical points:

First, employ best practices. Congregations have a long history of perpetuating ineffective practices, either because they were deemed ideologically correct or because they served the privileged needs of a certain subset. Either way, pursuing poor practices and expecting them to have anything other than poor results is foolish.

Second, aim for transparency. People tend to support what they helped to create, and they will adapt to changing circumstances if they understand what is changing and why. On the other hand, when change is imposed and when reasons and expected outcomes are hidden, people stop trusting and become hostile. Rather than resent that reaction by constituents, leaders should examine their own behavior.

Third, embrace outcome-based decision making. Church leaders need to drop their expectation that they will be given a "free pass" on outcomes, that they can do any old thing, not worry about results, and expect praise for trying. It is irresponsible stewardship to squander a church's resources. The enemy isn't failure. Failure is a sign of trying, and failure is generally a better teacher than success. The enemy is a refusal to acknowledge failure and to learn from failure. The enemy is a refusal to measure outcomes and to be guided by outcomes.

Wellness doesn't prevent the normal life cycles that any living entity will experience. Ideas run their course; programs rise and fall; people mature and age; congregations go through predictable cycles and do so within complex environments (neighborhoods, cities, cultures, nations) that themselves are going through life cycles.

Wellness doesn't guarantee success, prevent suffering, or alleviate anxiety. Wellness provides the foundation for taking risks, for dealing with pain, loss, grief, and illness, and for giving the anxious a place to bring their travail. The sign of wellness isn't a sea of smiles, but a community of compassionate, confident, and hopeful souls who are bending their lives to each other and, thus, to God.